To Read is to Fly

Flights of Fact and Fancy

Stories imbued with scientific exploration and discovery for children, youth and adults.

FAMILY READING

SUPPLEMENTAL CLASSROOM READING

READING FOR PLEASURE, SCIENCE AND NATURE

A bibliography of selected classic, award winning and new author story books, poetry and play scripts for all ages - children, teens, young and old adults - created to foster a love of reading and, through reading, a lifelong interest in science and nature and an understanding of the ways in which they affect our lives and, in turn, how our lives influence and change our world.

Books are the plane, and the train, and the road.
They are the destination, and the journey.
They are home.

—ANNA QUINDLEN

PUBLISHED BY

3 DOGS

216 F STREET, #25, DAVIS, CALIFORNIA 95616, USA
3dogspublishing@gmail.com

Printed in the USA
ISBN: 978-0-692-13341-5
Text Copyright © 2017 by Anne Hance
First Printing 2018

ANNE HANCE, *Author*
KAREN ADAIR, DG Creative Branding, *Design*
JOHN DAVENPORT, RBSA, *Illustrator*

Many grateful thanks to Karen Adair for her inspired design, John C. Davenport for his incredible illustrations, to Evelyn Buddenhagen, Lars Anderson, and Patty Shade for their important contributions to the process of creating the bibliography and to a host of others who made helpful suggestions. It took a full team to build *To Read Is To Fly.* —Thank you all!

ANNE HANCE, *the creator of this bibliography, has been a high school science teacher, a co-founder of the Explorit Science Center in Davis California, the Center's executive director for ten years, a board member for thirty plus years, and is the mother of three boys who love books.*

DAVIS, CALIFORNIA, U.S.A.
May 2018

Dear Reader,

This little book of books is for you to choose from when you are looking for something new to read.

The poet David McCord wrote a poem about books that starts like this,

> *"Books fall open*
> *you fall in,*
> *delighted where*
> *you've never been;*
> *...*
> *find unexpected*
> *keys to things*
> *locked up beyond imaginings."*

> And another famous poet, Gwendolyn Brooks, said,
> *"Books are meat and medicine*
> *and flame and flight and flower,*
> *steel, stitch, and cloud and clout,*
> *and drumbeats on the air."*

Our booklist has suggestions of some wonderful books for you to read (or have read to you) all with fine stories and illustrations to help you 'find unexpected things locked up beyond imaginings.' As you read we hope you will find that the nature and science in the stories is fascinating and will make you want to know more.

Browse our list, find some likely titles, and then look for the books in your local lending library or a neighborhood bookshop.

Read, enjoy and learn.

TABLE OF CONTENTS

INTRODUCTION

A blank page stares back. Like a book that has not been read. Both could reveal hidden worlds with the potency of words. A writer can transform the blank page into a complex of worlds within universes, of social ecosystems intertwined between pasts and presents, of landscapes both intimate and distant.

Reading those transformed pages can be for pleasure, entertainment, enlightenment. It is also a transport system to worlds beyond the pages, where dwell those things that we do not yet know, or dare not know.

Reading about something new can lead to unexpected destinations. As a teenager, I read The *Cry and the Covenant*, a fictionalized biography, published in 1949, of Ignaz Semmelweis who, in the late 19th century, struggled to understand why many women were dying from puerperal fever. He made the startling observation that more women died after they were visited by medical students than by midwives. His investigations revealed that something deadly was being spread from patient to patient by medical students. His rigorous protocol of hand washing before examining each patient was met with vehement resistance. Nevertheless, where hand washing was done, the deaths from puerperal fever dropped dramatically. The book describes his painful professional and personal quests to have his theory accepted until the tragic end of his life at age 47.

This was a stirring book for a young woman whose mind was

eager to know about the processes that link curiosity, unanswered questions, the power of observations, experimental theories, and, ultimately, solutions. That book lead to more books on similar subjects, more biographies that told of quests with monumental impact on human lives.

Ultimately, the impressionable teen years of reading such powerful books took me into laboratories and lectures at university where I ultimately chose to study microbiology, the field that was not yet born to Semmelweis when he followed his powers of observations.

A single book. A life transformed. This bibliography could play similar roles in enticing readers to transform ways of thinking, and, perhaps, even the direction of another young life.

It can be exhilarating to read books of science and nature as exemplified in this enticing bibliography. Pages are festooned with the banners of explorers who have explored the mysteries and wonders of other worlds, in the vast spaces of skies and seas, the micro spheres of earth, the intricate machinery that lies beneath skin, the towering diversity of chlorophyll-laden organisms, all nestled in stories for the curious.

This particular bibliography, lovingly compiled by its impassioned author, gives quick glimpses into select books, some with the science clearly on the pages and others with the science subtly embedded in the story, to invite relationships with books not yet read.

These books can create a harmony from a cacophony of endless questions that demand robust answers. If not harmony, then a healthy tension and restless search for more—more stories and more science.

Evelyn Buddenhagen
Microbiologist, teacher, reader and scientist for life

FOREWORD

    The *To Read Is To Fly* list is intended to be helpful to children as they search for story books to read for pleasure; and to their parents who can make choices for the youngest and provide guidance in the choices of older readers; and to teachers who are looking for supplemental general science reading story books to suggest to their students.

    A list of 100+ such books cannot possibly include all the books worthy of inclusion and so this one is meant as a catalyst to encourage further exploration at libraries and bookstores to find books that can help build and reinforce an awareness and familiarity with science as it relates to all aspects of our lives.

    But Wait! What is a "story" anyway?

    Stories are our way of sharing and preserving our histories, cultures, speculations, opinions and other such information about ourselves and our world. This little booklet aims to help connect story-readers with science and nature fact and fancy.

    Today the word "story" changes meaning depending on who is talking. A journalist writing an opinion piece or a factual account of an event, or an academic writing a report, may describe what they are writing as "stories." Storytelling techniques are also used to make children's textbooks more interesting to study. These sorts of stories have not been selected for inclusion here.

    In this bibliography the "stories" are of various kinds, mostly fiction. Whatever term has been chosen to define a book chosen for this publication they all have science overtly part of the story or subtly embedded, the writing and illustrations are high quality, and the science content and message are valid, engaging and timeless.

Let's amplify that explanation a bit by looking at what the terms mean as far as this bibliography is concerned. Fiction will be novels or short stories that deal imaginatively with people and their actions and experiences through a connected sequence of events. The author's own imagination creates the places where the story happens, the plot, the characters and the conversations. On the other hand, fact-based fiction is loosely based on real events or people.

What about nonfiction? These stories are based on real-life events, and factual science information. In this category biographies are personal life stories written by someone else. They may tell most of or only part of their subject's life through careful research using imaginative re-creations of scenes and events, and invented conversations. Autobiographies are life stories or selected personal experiences written by the author of his or her own life story. Narrative nonfiction is text that gets factual information across in a form that uses many of the elements of storytelling. True stories are written like novels or short stories. The author either lived through or has researched the events and re-creates scenes and experiences keeping the story as accurate as possible.

The titles selected to include in are general literature stories –old and new, classic and award winning. They are all waiting to be read and enjoyed.

ᴀND ABOUT READING...

"Since the age of five I had been one of those people who was an indefatigable reader, more inclined to go off by myself with a book than do any of the dozens of things that children usually do to amuse themselves. I never aged out of it."

-ANNA QUINDLEN, *IMAGINED LONDON*

Writing, the essential precursor to reading, evolved over thousands of years from simple stylistic characters marked on clay tablets or papyrus and conveying brief, simple messages, to our twenty-first century's complex systems of symbols, letters, printed on pages of paper.

In our society, print materials such as books can give a lifetime of pleasure, entertainment and learning and can assume a vital role in a reader's life. The book-reading can be solitary or shared. Belief in the value of reading to young children dates to the early 1900's when educators theorized that reading to youngsters was beneficial in developing literacy skills. They suggested too that what the reader and child talk about in the interaction holds the key to the effects of the storybook reading with the reader becoming a model to be emulated consciously or subconsciously.

I don't remember being read to but someone must have helped

me learn to read because I was a good reader by the age of 5 or 6. I dwelt within each book that I read. For that time period and beyond, as Robert Louis Stevenson wrote in the poem "My Kingdom":

This was the world and I was king;
For me the bees came by to sing;
For me the swallows flew.

This has evolved as I have become an adult. My self-absorption in a story has become less intense and I tend to be more aware of a writer's style, of the syntax, the vocabulary, the implied issues and other undertones of the story. The physical presence of a printed book, its look, smell, heft, choice of font and illustration, is perhaps more important to me though. Books are personal to me, each one to be judged according to my need or mood. I can easily put down a physical book that does not appeal to my sense of aesthetics.

But, although we generally ascribe the meaning of 'reading' to be the deciphering of written words or symbols, the necessary mental exercise is not restricted to a printed page. It is practiced too in the deciphering of man made or natural signs. Think of the zoologist who reads the spoor of animals in the forest or the subtleties of bird song; of the limnologist who reads the markings on a seashell. Think of an audience that reads the symbolism of a dancer's movements on the stage or of a piece of music, and the viewer who contemplates a work of art. They recognize and decode visual or aural messages associated with each activity just as a book reader decodes the words and their meanings represented by the writing on a page. Many of the stories listed here provide examples of the problem solving skills needed for such deciphering.

Finally, relevant to the science and nature themes within the stories of this booklist, anthropologist Philippe Descola asserts that in non-literate societies there tends to be little division between nature and culture while in literate (civilized) societies there is a nature/culture divide in which, as societies, we have tended to separate ourselves from nature —the animal and plant life of the countryside. Perhaps childhood and adult reading of books such as are listed in this bibliography can help to reunite us with our natural world.

For those adult readers who want to read more about books and reading:

- *Reading Like a Writer,* by Francine Prose (2007)
- *A History Of Reading,* by Alberto Manguel (2014)
- *A Reader on Reading,* by Alberto Manguel (2011)
- *Through the Magic Door,* by Arthur Conan Doyle (1907)
- *The Man Who Loved Books Too Much,* by Allison Hoover Bartlett (2010)
- *Daemon Voices: Essays on Storytelling,* by Philip Pullman (2017)
- *I'd Rather be Reading,* by Anne Bogel (2018)
- *The Bookshop Book,* by Jen Campbell (2015)
- *The Book Addict: Stories of Bibliomania,* by David Christopher Lane (2016)
- *The Book: An Homage,* by Burkhard Spinnen (2018)
- *The Library,* by Stuart Kells (2017)
- *The Library at Night,* by Alberto Manguel (2009)
- *The Book*: *A Cover-to-Cover Exploration of the Most Powerful Object of Our Time,* by Keith Houston (2016)
- *The Book: An Homage,* by Burkhard Spinnen (2018)

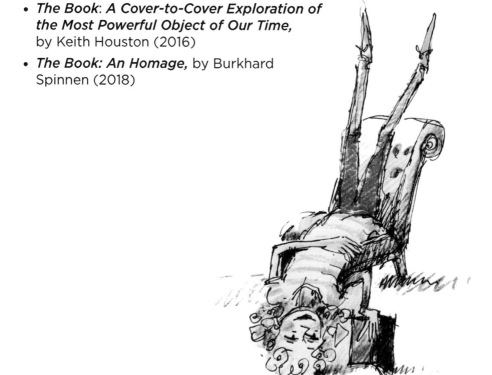

How are the Books Selected?

1. Well-written stories.

2. Valid science and nature content relevant to the story.

3. Characters in the story exhibit (especially in the 'mystery' codes and puzzles theme) behaviors including curiosity, questioning, investigation, analysis, critical thinking and problem solving.

4. Stories with positive human values.

How Are the Book Lists Arranged?

Assigning age range and grade level to a book is an inexact science; the suggestions given in this list are just that–suggestions. Individuals in all age categories vary widely in interest and reading competence.

Here is a guide but be aware that a very early reader might love looking at an adult book to enjoy the illustrations or to look for familiar word shapes. An adult might just love children's books. Included are books for all ages and most science and nature interests. What they all have in common is that they are well written literature, well illustrated and chosen for these attributes as well as their content.

Early Readers [1]: Ages 5-8, grades K-2 —Stories with themes written for young children with developing reading skills.

Intermediate Readers [2]: Ages 8-12, grades 3-6 —Stories with more involved subject matter, requiring good reading skills and some maturity.

Proficient Readers [3]: Ages 10-13, grades 4-7 —Stories with complex plots and themes, requiring proficient reading skills and maturity.

Advanced Readers [4]: Adult and Young Adult stories suitable for ages 14 and up, grades 8 and up. —Stories with more complicated plots and themes, demanding excellent reading skills and maturity. Likely to contain abstract, ironic, and/or figurative language. Moderate levels of discipline-specific content knowledge may be helpful.

SCIENCE GRAPHIC NOVELS: Ages 12 and up, grades 7 and up. —Fiction and nonfiction stories in comic format. These books may also appeal to adults.

POETRY BOOKS: Ages 4 and up. Poems written by famous poets as well as by other poets and by science educators. Most will be enjoyed by adults.

PLAY SCRIPTS: There are relatively few professionally written and performed play scripts that integrate science into the story and are suitable for children or young adults to read with comfort. The handful included here should be appropriate for young adult readers of 15 years and up.

CHILDREN'S MAGAZINES: A selection of children's subscription magazines that regularly include science articles. Most have both print and digital versions.

Footnote
In addition to the suggested age range and grade level for each book some books listed here include the Lexile text measure. This measure, written as a simple number followed by an "L" (e.g. 750L), indicates the difficulty of the text but not the book's content or quality. Not all books have yet been assigned Lexile measures, nor have all school students been tested to determine their Lexile reading ability

Books Listed by Category and Title

Age Range and Grade Level assignations are suggestions.

*Individuals in all age categories vary widely
in interest and reading competence.*

Early Readers [1]

**Ages 5-8 yrs, grades K-2; stories with themes written for
young children with developing reading skills. 25 Titles**

_____*Ada Twist Scientist,* by Andrea Beaty and David Roberts —
Fiction [1]

_____*Curious Garden, The,* by Peter Brown — Fiction [1]

_____*Dear Greenpeace,* by Simon James — Fiction Picture Book [1]

_____*Flying Girl, The: How Aida de Acosta Learned to Soar,* by
Margarita Engle — Fiction, True Story [1]

_____*Follow the Moon Home: A Tale of One Idea, Twenty Kids, and a
Hundred Sea Turtles,* by Phillippe Cousteau and Deborah
Hopkinson — Narrative Nonfiction [1]

_____*Humblebee Hunter, The,* by Deborah Hopkinson — Fiction [1]

_____*Joan Procter, Dragon Doctor: The Woman Who Loved Reptiles,*
by Patricia Valdez —Biography [1]

_____*Lorax, The,* by Theodore Seuss — Fiction [1]

_____*Mary Anning and The Sea Dragon,* by Jeannine Atkins — Fiction,
True Story [1]

_____*Mighty, Mighty Construction Site,* by Sherri Duskey Rinker —
Fiction [1]

_____*Moon is Made of Cheese, The,* by Chris and Jenny Kjorness — Fiction [1]

_____*My Journey to the Stars,* by Scott Kelly — Autobiography [1]

_____*On a Beam of Light: A Story of Albert Einstein,* by Jennifer Berne — Biography, [1]

_____*Orcas Around Me,* by Debra Page — True Story [1].

_____*Outside Your Window: A First Book of Nature,* by Nicola Davies — Fiction Picture Book [1]

_____*Over and Under the Snow,* by Kate Messner (2011) Fiction [1]

_____*Rosie Revere, Engineer,* by Andrea Beaty and David Roberts — Fiction [1]

_____*Shark Lady,* by Jess Keating — True Story [1]

_____*Snowflake Bentley,* by Jacqueline Briggs Martin — Fiction, True Story [1]

_____*Turtle, Turtle, Watch Out!,* by April Pulley Sayre — Fiction, Picture Storybook [1]

_____*Weed Is a Flower, A The Life of George Washington Carver,* by Aliki — True Story [1]

_____*Who Sank the Boat?,* by Pamela Allen — Fiction [1]

_____*Who Says Women Can't Be Computer Programmers?: The Story of Ada Lovelace,* by Tanya Lee Stone — Biography [1]

_____*Wild Woods, The,* by Simon James — Fiction [1]

_____*Winter is Coming,* by Tony Johnston — Fiction [1]

Intermediate Readers [2]

Ages 8-12, grades 3-6

Stories with more involved subject matter requiring good reading skills and some maturity. 42 Titles

____*Ada Lovelace, Poet of Science: The First Computer Programmer,* by Diane Stanley — Biographical [2]

____*Adam's Atomic Adventures,* by Alice Baxter — Fiction [2]

____*Beetle Boy,* by M G Leonard — Fiction [2]

____*Blue John's Cavern: Time Travel Rocks!,* by Tracy Barnhart — Adventure Fiction [2]

____*Boy Who Harnessed The Wind, The: Young Readers' Edition,* by William Kamkwamba — True Story [2]

____*Brilliant Fall of Gianna Z., The,* by Kate Messner — Fiction [2]

____*Charlotte's Web,* by E.B. White — Fiction [2]

____*Clockwork or All Wound Up,* by Philip Pullman — Fantasy Fiction [2]

____*Countdown Conspiracy, The,* by Katie Slivensky — Mystery Fiction [2]

____*Dinosaur Hunters,* by Catherine Chambers —Fiction [2]

____*Dinosaurs Before Dark,* by Mary Pope Osborne —Fiction [2]

____*Earth Dragon Awakes, The: The San Francisco Earthquake of 1906,* by Laurence Yep —Fact-based Fiction [2]

____*Escape from Mr. Lemoncello's Library,* by Chris Grabenstein — Fiction [2]

____*Feather Chase, The,* by Shannon L. Brown — Fiction [2]

____*Firework Maker's Daughter, The,* by Philip Pullman — Fantasy Fiction [2]

____*Frankie Files, The,* by A. J. Ponder — Fiction [2]

____*Galileo's Journal: 1609–1610* by Jeanne Pettenati — Fact-based Fiction [2]

____*George's Secret Key to the Universe,* by Stephen Hawking and Lucy Hawking — Adventure Fiction [2]

____*Girls Who Looked Under Rocks,* by Jeanine Atkins and Paula Conner — True Stories [2]

_____*Itch,* by Simon Mayo — Adventure Fiction [2]

_____*Longleaf,* by Roger Reid — Adventure Fiction [2]

_____*Matilda,* by Roald Dahl — Fiction [2]

_____*Nefertiti, the Spidernaut: The Jumping Spider Who Learned to Hunt in Space,* by Darcy Patterson — Narrative Nonfiction, True Story [2]

_____*One and Only Ivan, The,* by Katherine Applegate — True Story [2]

_____*Rare Treasure: Mary Anning and Her Remarkable Discoveries,* by Don Brown — Fiction, True Story [2]

_____*Riptide,* by Frances Ward Weller — Fact-based Fiction [2],

_____*Scarecrow and his Servant, The,* by Philip Pullman — Fairytale Fiction [2]

_____*Silverwing,* by Kenneth Oppel — Nature Fiction [2]

_____*Stuart Little,* by E.B. White — Fiction [2]

_____*Summer of the Monkeys,* by Wilson Rawls — Adventure Fction [2]

_____*Swallows and Amazons,* by Arthur Ransome — Fiction [2]

_____*Time,* by Roger Reid — Adventure Fiction [2]

_____*Tin Snail, The,* by Cameron McAllister — Fiction [2]

_____*Tom's Midnight Garden,* by Philippa Pearce — Fantasy Fiction [2]

_____*Treasure,* (Seed Savers Book 1) by S. Smith — Fiction [2]

_____*Tricking the Tallyman,* by Jacqueline Davies — Fiction [2]

_____*Trumpet of the Swan,* by E.B. White — Fiction [2]

_____*Vincent Shadow: Toy Inventor,* by Tim Kehoe — Fiction [2]

_____*When You Reach Me,* by Rebecca Stead —Fiction [2]

_____*Who Really Killed Cock Robin?,* by Jean Craighead George — Fiction [2]

_____*Wild Robot, The,* by Peter Brown — Fiction [2]

_____*Wild Wings,* by Gill Lewis — Fiction [2]

_____*Wisdom, the Midway Albatross,* by Darcy Pattison — Narrative Nonfiction, True Story [2]

_____*Wonderful Flight to the Mushroom Planet, The,* by Eleanor Cameron — Fantasy Fiction [2]

Proficient Readers [3]

Ages 10-13 grades 4-7 stories with complex plots and themes, requiring proficient reading skills and maturity.
56 Titles

_____*Admiral Richard Byrd: Alone in the Antarctic,* by Paul Rink — Biography [3]

_____*Beyond the Bright Sea,* by Lauren Wolk — Fiction [3]

_____*Book Scavenger, The,* by Jennifer Chambliss Bertman — Fiction [3]

_____*Born Free,* by Joy Adamson — True Story [3]

_____*Case of the Missing Moonstone, The,* (The Wollstonecraft Detective Agency, Book 1) by Jordan Stratford — Fiction [3]

_____*Charlie's Raven,* by Jean Craighead George — Nature Fiction [3]

_____*Chasing Vermeer,* by Blue Balliett —Fiction [3]

_____*Dragon Bones and Dinosaur Eggs,* by Ann Bausum — True Story [3]

_____*Every Living Thing,* by James Herriot — Fact-based Fiction [3]

_____*Evolution of Calpurnia Tate, The,* by Jacqueline Kelly — Fiction [3]

_____*Eye of the Storm,* by Kate Messner — Suspenseful Fiction [3]

_____*Finding the Lone Woman of San Nicolas Island,* by R.C. Nidever — True Story [3]

_____*Fourteenth Goldfish, The,* by Jennifer L. Holm — Fiction [3]

_____*Fuzzy Mud,* by Louis Sachar — Science Mystery Fiction [3]

_____*Gebra Named A, Al,* by Wendy Isdell — Fantasy Fiction [3]

_____*Great Trouble, The: A Mystery of London, the Blue Death, and a Boy Called Eel,* by Deborah Hopkinson — Fact-based Fiction [3]

_____*Hatchet,* by Gary Paulsen — Fiction [3]

_____*Hoot,* by Carl Hiassen — Ecological Mystery Fiction [3]

_____*House of the Scorpion, The,* by Nancy Farmer — Science Fiction [3]

_____*In The Shadow of Man,* by Jane Goodall — Autobiographical [3]

_____*Isaac The Alchemist: Secrets of Isaac Newton, Reveal'd,* by Mary Losure — Biographical [3]

_____*Island of the Blue Dolphins,* by Scott O'Dell — True Story Novel [3]

_____*Island of the Unknowns: A Mystery,* by Benedict Carey — Fiction [3]

_____*Jack and the Geniuses, At the Bottom of the World,* by Bill Nye and Gregory Mone — Adventure Fiction [3]

_____*Julie of the Wolves,* by Jean Craighead George — Nature Fiction [3]

_____*Kine,* by A. R. Lloyd — Nature Fiction [3]

_____*Life on Surtsey: Iceland's Upstart Island,* by Loree Burns — Narrative Nonfiction, True Story [3]

_____*Mary Andromeda and the Amazing Eye,* by J.G. Kemp — Fiction [3]

_____*Miscalculations of Lightning Girl, The,* by Stacy McAnuity — Fiction [3]

_____*Mrs. Frisby and the Rats of NIMH,* by Robert C. O'Brien — Fiction [3]

_____*My Family and Other Animals,* by Gerald Durrell — Autobiography [3]

_____*My Season with Penguins: An Antarctic Journal,* by Sophie Webb — Narrative Nonfiction, True Story [3]

_____*My Side of the Mountain,* by Jean Craighead George — Adventure Fiction [3]

_____*My Sister Rosalind Franklin: A Family Memoir,* by Jenifer Glynn — Biography [3]

_____*Mysterious Benedict Society, The,* by Trenton Lee Stewart — Fiction [3]

_____*Never Cry Wolf,* by Farley Mowat — Fiction, True Story [3]

_____*New World of Mr. Tompkins, The,* by George Gamow and Russell Stannard — Physics Fiction [3]

_____*Pax,* by Sara Pennypacker — Fiction [3]

_____*Phantom Tollbooth, The,* by Norton Juster — Fantasy Fiction [3]

_____*Privileged Hands: A Scientific Life,* by Geerat Vermeij — Autobiography [3]

_____*Project Mulberry Park,* by Linda Sue Park — Fiction [3]

_____*Rise of the Rocket Girls,* by Nathalia Holt — True Stories [3]

_____*River Singers, The,* by Tom Moorhouse — Fiction [3]

_____*Rocket Boys,* (The Coalwood Series #1) by Homer Hickam — True Story, Memoir [3]

_____*Sea Otter Heroes: The Predators That Saved an Ecosystem,* by Patricia Newman — Narrative Nonfiction, True Story [3]

_____*Seedfolks,* by Paul Fleischman — Fiction [3]

_____*Sweetness at the Bottom of the Pie, The,* by Alan Bradley — Mystery Fiction [3]

_____*Tales from Watership Down,* by Richard Adams — Fiction [3]

_____*There's a Hair in My Dirt,* by Gary Larson — Fiction [3]

_____*Time and Space of Uncle Albert, The,* by Russell Stannard — Fiction [3]

_____*Town Secrets (The Book of Adam 1),* by Scott Gelowitz — Fiction [3]

_____*Under the Egg,* by Laura Mars Fitzgerald — Fiction [3]

_____*Untamed: The Wild Life of Jane Goodall,* by Anita Silvey, Foreword by Jane Goodall — Biography [3]

_____*Water Sky,* by Jean Craighead George — Fiction [3]

_____*Way We Fall, The,* by Megan Crew — Fiction [3]

_____*Westing Game, The,* by Ellen Raskin — Fiction [3]

_____*What Color Is My World?,* by Kareem Abdul-Jabbar — Fact-based Fiction [3]

_____*Wrinkle in Time, A,* by Madeline L'Engle — Fantasy Fiction [3]

Advanced Readers [4]

Adult and Young Adult Stories suitable
for ages 14 and to adult, grades 8 and up. 35 Titles

*Includes stories with more complicated plots and themes,
demanding excellent reading skills and maturity. Likely to contain
abstract, ironic, and/or figurative language. Moderate levels of
discipline-specific content knowledge may be helpful.*

_____*3:59,* by Gretchen McNeil — Science Fiction [4]

_____*40 Signs of Rain,* by Kim Stanley Robinson — Fiction [4]

_____*Airborn,* by Kenneth Oppel — Steampunk Fiction [4]

_____*An Abundance of Katherines,* by John Green — Mathematics
Fiction [4]

_____*Archangel,* by Andrea Barrett — Fiction, Short Stories [4]

_____*Ashfall,* by Mike Mullin — Fiction [4]

_____*Billion Dollar Molecule, The, One Company's Quest for the
Perfect Drug,* by Barry Werth — Nonfiction [4+]

_____*Boat Who Wouldn't Float, The,* by Farley Mowat — True Story
Novel [4]

_____*Certain Ambiguity, A: A Mathematical Novel,* by Gaurav Suri and
Hartosh Bal — Mathematical Fiction [4]

_____*Double Helix, The,* by James D. Watson — True Story Memoir [4]

_____*Elephant Whisperer, The,* by Lawrence Anthony — True Story
Novel [4]

_____*Flatland: A Romance of Many Dimensions,* by Edwin Abbott
— Mathematics Fiction [4]

_____*Galileo's Daughter,* by Dava Stobel — Biographical Fiction [4]

_____*Hidden Figures,* by Margot Lee Shetterly — Fact-based Fiction
[4]

_____*King Solomon's Ring,* by Konrad Lorenz — Nonfiction [4]

_____*Lab Girl,* by Hope Jahren — Autobiographical [4]

_____*Last Days of Night, The,* by Graham Moore — Fact-based Fiction
[4]

_____*Life As We Knew It,* by Susan Beth Pfeffer —Science Fiction Novel
[4]

_____**Man Meets Dog,** by Konrad Lorenz — Nonfiction [4]

_____**Martian, The,** by Andy Weir — Science Fiction [4]

_____**Microbe Hunters,** by Paul de Kruif — Fact-based Fiction [4]

_____**Passion for Science, A,** by Lewis Wolpert and Alison Richards — Nonfiction [4]

_____**Petroplague,** by Amy Rogers — Fiction [4]

_____**Practice Effect, The,** by David Brin — Science Fiction [4]

_____**Rats,** by Robert Sullivan — True Story [4]

_____**Seeds: A post-apocalyptic adventure,** by Chris Mandeville — Science Fiction [4]

_____**Servants of the Map,** by Andrea Barrett — Fiction, Short Stories [4]

_____**Shell Collector, The,** by Anthony Doerr (2001) — Fiction, Short Stories [4]

_____**Ship Breaker,** by Paolo Bacigalupi — Adventure Fiction [4]

_____**Ship Fever,** by Andrea Barrett — Fiction, Short Stories [4]

_____**Story of Charlotte's Web,** by Michael Sims — Nonfiction [4]

_____**Uncle Tungsten,** by Oliver Sacks — Autobiographical [4]

_____**Voyage of the Narwhal, The,** by Andrea Barrett — Fiction [4]

_____**Watership Down,** by Richard Adams — Fiction [4]

_____**Wizard of Quarks, The,** by Robert Gilmore — Fantasy fiction, Physics [4]

"What an astonishing thing a book is. It's a flat object, made from a tree, with flexible parts on which are imprinted lots of funny dark squiggles. But one glance at it and you're inside the mind of another person ... an author is speaking clearly and silently inside your head, directly to you. Writing is perhaps the greatest of human inventions, binding together people who never knew each other, citizens of distant epochs. Books break the shackles of time. A book is proof that humans are capable of working magic."

—CARL SAGAN, COSMOS

BOOK DESCRIPTIONS

EARLY READER STORIES

ADA TWIST SCIENTIST, BY ANDREA BEATY AND DAVID ROBERTS
(2017) FICTION [1]
AGE RANGE 5-7 / GRADE LEVEL K-2 / 550L /
THEME: QUESTIONING AND EXPERIMENTATION

A story about the power of curiosity in the hands of a child who is
on a mission to use science to understand her world. Ada Twist,
Scientist is a celebration of STEM, perseverance, and passion. Ada, a
young girl of color, has a boundless imagination and has always
been hopelessly curious. She embarks on fact-finding missions and
conducts scientific experiments, all in the name of discovery. But her
experiments lead into trouble!
NOTES: _____

CURIOUS GARDEN, THE, BY PETER BROWN (2009) FICTION,
PICTURE STORYBOOK [1]
AGE RANGE 5-7 / GRADE LEVEL K-2 / 840L / THEME: GARDENING,
BOTANY

One boy's quest for a greener world, one garden at a time. Environmental themes and delightful illustrations. Redheaded Liam can be
spotted on every page as he works to grow the plants and create a
garden. This adds a seek-and-find element.
NOTES: _____

DEAR GREENPEACE, BY SIMON JAMES (1991) FICTION PICTURE
BOOK [1]
AGE RANGE 4-7 / GRADE LEVEL K-2 / THEME: ECOLOGY

An ecological fantasy, Dear Greenpeace is a told in letters to Greenpeace from a little girl who is worried about the whale that is living
in her pond. Through her correspondence exchange with Greenpeace, Emily learns a lot about whales while Greenpeace insists
there couldn't possibly be a whale in Emily's pond.

NOTES: _____

**FLYING GIRL, THE: HOW AIDA DE ACOSTA LEARNED TO
SOAR,** BY MARGARITA ENGLE (2018) TRUE STORY [1]
AGE RANGE 4 - 8 YEARS / GRADE LEVEL PRESCHOOL – 3 / THEME:
POWERED FLIGHT

In this beautiful picture book award-winners Margarita Engle and
Sara Palacios tell the true story of Frenchwoman Aída de Acosta, the
first woman to fly a motorized aircraft.

As a nineteen-year-old in 1903, on a street in the city of Paris, teenager Aída glanced up to see an airship and wished she could soar
through the sky like that! The inventor of the airship, aviator Alberto
Santos-Dumont, invited Aída to ride with him, but she didn't want to
be a passenger. She wanted to be the pilot. She took three flight
lessons, before taking to the sky by herself and embarking upon a
one and a half hours solo flight in Dumont's personal dirigible.

NOTES: _____

**FOLLOW THE MOON HOME: A TALE OF ONE IDEA,
TWENTY KIDS, AND A HUNDRED SEA TURTLES,** BY
PHILLIPPE COUSTEAU AND DEBORAH HOPKINSON (2016) FICTION [1]
AGE RANGE 6-8 / GRADE LEVEL 1-3 / 520L / THEME: BIOLOGY, SEA
TURTLES, CONSERVATION

The story provides an excellent example of how kids can make a
difference through careful research, critical thinking, and problem
solving. As a class project the students in Vivienne's new school are
looking for a problem to solve and they discover that the baby
loggerhead sea turtles that are about to hatch on the local South
Carolina beach may need help making it down to the ocean. Bright
watercolor illustrations chronicle each stage of the children's efforts
to involve the community in their project.

NOTES: _____

HUMBLEBEE HUNTER, THE, BY DEBORAH HOPKINSON (2010)
FICTION [1]
AGE RANGE 4-8 / GRADE LEVEL 1-4 / 610L / THEME: BIOLOGY, BEES,
SCIENCE INQUIRY

An imaginative tale about the family of Charles Darwin told from
daughter Etty's point of view. Etty joins her father and her siblings
as they observe the habits of the "humblebees" (bumblebees).
Hopkinson imagines using a drift of flour to mark the bees so that
each child can follow a bee from flower to flower to calculate how
many visits it makes per minute. The method is fiction but we know
that Darwin did enlist his children's help in observing bees in their
garden.

NOTES: _____

JOAN PROCTER, DRAGON DOCTOR: THE WOMAN WHO LOVED REPTILES, BY PATRICIA VALDEZ (2018) BIOGRAPHY [1]
AGE RANGE 4-8 / GRADE LEVEL PRESCHOOL – 3 / THEME: REPTILES

A picture book biography of a pioneering female scientist who loved
reptiles. While other girls played with dolls, Joan preferred the
company of her family of reptiles. She carried her favorite lizard with
her everywhere; she even took a crocodile to school. As an adult
Joan became the Curator of Reptiles at the British Museum and
went on to design the Reptile House at the London Zoo. Joan
Beauchamp Procter (1897 – 1931) was internationally recognized as
an outstanding herpetologist.

NOTES: _____

LORAX, THE, BY THEODOR SEUSS (1971) FICTION [1]
AGE RANGE 6-9 / GRADE LEVEL 1-4 / 560L / THEME: ECOLOGY

Dr. Seuss, speaking through his character the Lorax, warns against
mindless progress and the danger it poses to the earth's natural
beauty.

The Lorax is an ecological warning of the dangers of clear-cutting,
pollution, and disregard for the earth's environment. In The Lorax,
brilliantly whimsical rhymes, delightfully original creatures, and
weirdly undulating illustrations carry a message for both children
and adults.

NOTES: _____

MARY ANNING AND THE SEA DRAGON, BY JEANNINE ATKINS
(2012) FICTION, TRUE STORY [1]
AGE RANGE 6-8 YEARS / GRADE LEVEL 1-3 / 560L / THEME:
DISCOVERY, FOSSILS

Over two hundred years ago, in Dorset, England, eleven-year-old
Mary Anning discovered a different sort of fossil, the first complete
dinosaur fossil 'ichthyosaurus', or 'fish-lizard' ever seen. This began a
lifelong vocation that made Mary famous and has earned her a place
in history as a geologist (a paleontologist). Atkins presents a roman-
ticized portrait of the discovery of the fossil. For the 6-7 year-old
beginning readers this story will make a great read-aloud book. The
book *Rare Treasure: Mary Anning and Her Remarkable Discoveries*
by Don Brown (included in this bibliography) for a slightly older
reader contains more detailed science information.

NOTES: _____

MIGHTY, MIGHTY CONSTRUCTION SITE, BY SHERRI DUSKEY
RINKER (2017) FICTION [1]
AGE RANGE 2–4 / GRADE LEVEL P-K /710L / THEME: CONSTRUCTION

A picture, storybook. The page filling drawings and text focus on
team-building, friendship, and working together to make a big task
seem small. Down in the big construction site the crew faces their
biggest job yet and will need the help of new construction friends to
get it done. Working as a team, there's nothing they can't do!

NOTES: _____

MOON IS MADE OF CHEESE, THE, BY CHRIS AND JENNY
KJORNESS (2016) FICTION [1]
AGE RANGE 5-7 / GRADE LEVEL K-2 / THEME: INVENTION

Milton is a mouse who loves to build things. He spends every day
working on new inventions and dreaming up adventures. This
slim-volume story is about invention, learning and grit. The Authors
Chris and Jenny Kjorness get ideas for books by watching their two
boys explore the world.

NOTES: _____

MY JOURNEY TO THE STARS, BY SCOTT KELLY (2017)
NONFICTION: AUTOBIOGRAPHICAL STORY [1]
AGE RANGE 5–8 / GRADE LEVEL K–3 / 680L / THEME: SPACE

NASA astronaut Scott Kelly was the first to spend an entire year in space! His awe-inspiring journey in this fascinating picture book memoir is a companion to his adult autobiographical book Endurance that takes readers from Scott's childhood as an average student to his record-breaking year among the stars.

NOTES: _____

ON A BEAM OF LIGHT: A STORY OF ALBERT EINSTEIN, BY JENNIFER BERNE (2016) BIOGRAPHY, [1]
AGE RANGE 6-8 YEARS / GRADE LEVEL 1–3 / 680L / THEME: FACT-BASED FICTION

It's not easy to explain the work of Albert Einstein to a young audience, but this book pulls it off and provides an overview of Einstein's life: the way he thought and how his remarkable ideas changed the way scientists think. The book reroutes the text around events in Einstein's life, such as his escape from Nazi Germany and his move to the U.S., and it only touches upon his work on the nuclear bomb. This is a more personal look, but still, it explains how he came to the discovery of atoms and his theories about the speed of light. The book stresses that readers may someday answer the questions that Einstein didn't get to.

NOTES: _____

ORCAS AROUND ME, BY DEBRA PAGE AND LESLIE W. BOWMAN (1997) FACT BASED FICTION [1].
AGE RANGE 5-8 / GRADES K-2 / 710L / THEME: NATURAL HISTORY, OCEAN ANIMALS

Young Taiga Page (named for Alaska's northern forest) is used as the narrator in this description of life along the north Pacific coast as his family trolls for salmon. In a series of anecdotes, Taiga provides verbal snapshots of his family at work: pumping the bilge, cleaning their catch, and meeting sea lions, porpoises, otters, and a cluster of orcas. He recalls humorous and scary moments, unobtrusively weaving bits of information into his account. The days are filled with unique and valuable interactions with the natural world. Leslie W. Bowman's attractive watercolors capture the Page family, their work, and the creatures they encounter.

NOTES: _____

OUTSIDE YOUR WINDOW: A FIRST BOOK OF NATURE, BY
NICOLA DAVIES (2012) PICTURE BOOK [1]
AGE RANGE 3-7 / GRADE LEVEL PRESCHOOL- 2 / THEME: NATURE

A book to evoke a child's first experience of nature. Poetic text cycles through the year from spring to winter. The verse offers observations and information about the natural world as well as reflections, short narratives, and suggestions to help children to enjoy it. This is a large format, lavishly illustrated book. Mark Hearld's pictures beautifully reproduce the colors of the seasons, and Nicola Davies' lyrical words capture the simple loveliness that is everywhere.

NOTES: _____

OVER AND UNDER THE SNOW, BY KATE MESSNER (2011)
NATURAL HISTORY FICTION [1]
AGE RANGE: 4-8 YEARS / GRADE LEVEL: KINDERGARTEN-2 / THEME: NATURE, HIBERNATION

Skiing through a snowy wood, a girl and her father watch for signs of animals and the little girl becomes aware of a secret kingdom beneath the snow. An easy reading story in which the dad and daughter talk about animals they see and the ones they don't see.

By the same author: *Up in the Garden and Down in the Dirt* (2015) and *Over and Under the Pond* (2017).

NOTES: _____

ROSIE REVERE, ENGINEER, BY ANDREA BEATY (2013) FICTION [1]
AGE RANGE 5-7 YEARS / GRADE LEVEL KINDERGARTEN-2 / 860L / THEME: INVENTION, PERSISTENCE

Rosie is a child inventor of gizmos and gadgets who dreams of becoming a great engineer. When her great-great-aunt Rose (Rosie the Riveter) comes for a visit and mentions that her goal is to fly, Rosie sets to work building a contraption to make her aunt's dream come true. But her contraption doesn't fly and Rosie deems it a failure. On the contrary, Aunt Rose insists that Rosie's contraption was a raging success. You can only truly fail, she explains, if you quit.

NOTES: _____

SHARK LADY: THE TRUE STORY OF HOW EUGENIE CLARK BECAME THE OCEAN'S MOST FEARLESS SCIENTIST, BY JESS KEATING (2017) FACT-BASED FICTION [1]
AGE RANGE 4-8 YEARS / GRADE LEVEL 1-4 / 730L / THEME: MARINE BIOLOGY, SHARKS

This is the story of a real person, a pioneer in marine conservation and the study of shark behavior, a woman who dared to dive, defy, discover, and inspire. Eugenie Clark fell in love with sharks from the first moment she saw them at the aquarium and devoted her life to learning about them. After earning several college degrees and making countless discoveries, Eugenie wrote herself into the history of science, earning the nickname "Shark Lady." The author, Jess Keating, is a zoologist. The book includes a timeline of Eugenie's life and many fin-tastic shark facts! Named a Best Children's Book of 2017 by Parents Magazine.

NOTES: _____

SNOWFLAKE BENTLEY, BY JACQUELINE BRIGGS MARTIN (1999) FICTION BASED ON FACT [1]
AGE RANGE 4-8 / GRADE LEVEL PRE-3 / 830L / THEME: PHYSICS, ICE, SNOW CRYSTALS

"Of all the forms of water the tiny six-pointed crystals of ice called snow are incomparably the most beautiful and varied." –Wilson Bentley.

This is the true story of a Vermont farm boy mesmerized by snow-flakes. From the time he was a small boy in Vermont, Wilson Bentley saw snowflakes as small miracles. His enthusiasm for photographing snowflakes revealed two important truths: no two snowflakes are alike; and each one is startlingly beautiful. His story gives children insight into a scientist's vision and perseverance and a passion for the wonders of nature. Snowflake Bentley won the 1999 Caldecott Medal.

NOTES: _____

TURTLE, TURTLE, WATCH OUT!, BY APRIL PULLEY SAYRE (2000) FICTION, PICTURE STORYBOOK [1]
AGE RANGE 5 TO 8 /GRADE LEVEL K–3 / 530L / THEME: NATURAL HISTORY, TURTLES

This is a picture book story about the cycle of life for a sea turtle. It addresses conservation and ecology and shows the types of dangers a sea turtle encounters on land and in the sea. The story follows one baby turtle that survives, matures, and returns one night to the same Florida beach to lay her own eggs and illustrates the role humans can play in helping these endangered turtles survive. Beautifully illustrated the story implicitly challenges children to be caretakers of wildlife.

NOTES: _____

WEED IS A FLOWER, A: THE LIFE OF GEORGE WASHINGTON CARVER, BY ALIKI (1965) TRUE STORY [1]
AGE RANGE 4-8 YEARS / GRADE LEVEL: PRESCHOOL – 3 / 640L / THEME: SCIENCE, AGRICULTURE

Brief text and pictures present the life of the man, born a slave, who became a scientist and devoted his life to helping improve agriculture. George Washington Carver (1860s –1943) was an American botanist and inventor. He became well known due to his active promotion of alternative crops to cotton and methods to prevent soil depletion.

NOTES: _____

WHO SANK THE BOAT?, BY PAMELA ALLEN (1983) FICTION
STORY PICTURE BOOK [1]
AGE RANGE 2-5 / GRADE LEVEL PRE-K–1 / 470L / THEME: PHYSICS CONCEPT.

The reader is invited to guess who causes the boat to sink when five animal friends of varying sizes—a cow, a donkey, a sheep, a pig and a mouse—try to clamber in one after the other. The illustrations are large, delightful and help with understanding the story. As a read-aloud story can lead to good conversation about sizes, weights and measures.

NOTES: _____

WHO SAYS WOMEN CAN'T BE COMPUTER PROGRAMMERS?: THE STORY OF ADA LOVELACE, BY
TANYA LEE STONE (2018) BIOGRAPHY [1]
AGE RANGE: 6-9 YEARS / GRADE LEVEL: 1-2 / THEME: COMPUTERS

A picture book biography of Ada Lovelace who is recognized today as history's first computer programmer. She was an Englishwoman variously known as Augusta Ada Gordon, Ada Byron, Ada Lovelace, and Augusta Ada King, Countess of Lovelace and lived in the early nineteenth century. The daughter of internationally acclaimed poet Lord Byron and his mathematical wife, Annabella, Ada was tutored in science and mathematics from a very early age and, armed with the fundamentals of math and engineering, she worked with Charles Babbage as he developed his Analytical Engine. Priceman illuminates the pages exuberantly with numbers, letters, and mathematical computations.

NOTES: _____

WILD WOODS, THE, BY SIMON JAMES (1993) FICTION [1]
AGE RANGE 5-7 / GRADE LEVEL K-2 / THEME: ECOLOGY

A heartwarming tale with an important ecological message about respecting an animal's natural habitat. Simon James is an award-winning author and illustrator of picture books for children; some pages are just pictures, with lots to see. A simple story told with loose and lively illustrations. The relationship between the child and her grandfather is captured, as is the fun to be had in exploration.

NOTES: _____

WINTER IS COMING, BY TONY JOHNSTON (2014) NONFICTION [1]
AGE RANGE 4–8 / GRADE LEVEL P–3 / 330L / THEME: CHANGING OF THE SEASONS

A picture storybook. Through delightful, page-filling pictures and easy to read narrative, witness the changing of a season through a watchful child's eyes in this story of nature and discovery from award-winning author Tony Johnston and New York Times Best Illustrated artist Jim La Marche. Day after day, a girl goes to her favorite place in the woods and quietly watches from her tree house as the chipmunks, the doe, the rabbits prepare for the winter. As the temperature drops, sunset comes earlier and a new season begins.

NOTES: _____

"The more that you read, the more things you will know. The more that you learn, the more places you'll go."
—DR. SEUSS

Intermediate Reader Stories

ADA LOVELACE, POET OF SCIENCE: THE FIRST COMPUTER PROGRAMMER, BY DIANE STANLEY (2016)
BIOGRAPHICAL [2]
AGE RANGE 9-11 YEARS / GRADE LEVEL 3-5 / 810L / THEME: BIOGRAPHY, EARLY COMPUTER PROGRAMMING

This is a lively, illustrated biography of Ada Lovelace, who is known as the first computer programmer. Ada was born two hundred years ago to the famous poet, Lord Byron, and his mathematical wife, Annabella. Like her mother, she had a passion for science, math, and machines. With her meticulous, step-by-step detail of how to code numbers she wrote the first computer program in partnership with mathematician Charles Babbage who invented the first mechanical computer. The text briefly touches upon such topics as the Industrial Revolution.

NOTES: _____

ADAM'S ATOMIC ADVENTURES, BY ALICE BAXTER (2007)
FICTION [2]
AGE RANGE 8-11 / GRADE LEVEL 3-6 / THEME: CHEMISTRY

Mrs. Gold, Adam's rather peculiar science teacher, makes him stay behind after class to share with him a startling secret: she's much more than a science teacher. Mrs. Gold is a powerful alchemist who's counting on Adam's help to save the world! Mrs. Gold has chosen Adam, one of her best students, for a critical task. She plans to shrink Adam down to the microscopic size of a single atom and send him to the Periodic School for the Elements to search for Ollie, a missing atom of oxygen. Alice L. Baxter taught chemistry for more than thirty years.

NOTES: _____

BEETLE BOY, BY M G LEONARD (2016) FICTION [2]
AGE RANGE 8 - 12 YEARS / GRADE LEVEL 3 – 7 / THEME: MYSTERY, INSECTS, BEETLES

Darkus's dad has disappeared - but his new friend, a giant beetle called Baxter, is some consolation. Together, boy and beetle set out to solve the mystery of his father's disappearance. In this, first book of a trilogy, Leonard gives readers a rare glimpse into the world of insects, mixing adventure, mystery, and science to create a story that's more than just a novel about bugs.

NOTES: _____

BLUE JOHN'S CAVERN, TIME TRAVEL ROCKS!, BY TRACY BARNHART (2017) ADVENTURE FICTION [2]
AGE RANGE 8-12 / GRADE LEVEL 3-6 / THEME: GEOLOGY

Local teenagers Emma and Brody don't know that their neighbor, a famous geologist, is about to show them the wildest time of their lives. Blue John's Cavern is the first book in the middle-grade adventure/sci-fi series Crystal Cave Adventures in which the two children learn about rocks and minerals, travel through caves, and jump through time.

Tracy Barnhart, geologist and author, was born and raised in Princeton, West Virginia. After working as an environmental consultant for many years, Tracy opened Mini Me Geology with her own line of rock and mineral kits designed for kids of all ages.

NOTES: _____

BOY WHO HARNESSED THE WIND, THE, YOUNG READER'S EDITION, BY WILLIAM KAMKWAMBA, (2012) TRUE STORY [2]
AGE RANGE 8-13 / GRADE LEVEL 4-7 / 860L / THEME: INVENTION

A remarkable true story about human inventiveness. This youth edition of the original adult book of the same title has been skillfully adapted for middle grade readers. Inventor William Kamkwamba and journalist Bryan Mealer collaborate with illustrator Elizabeth Zunon to masterfully share with the young reader the story of William's life in drought-ravaged Malawi and his ingenuity that inspired him to build a windmill that would affect his life and the lives of those around him.

NOTES: _____

BRILLIANT FALL OF GIANNA Z., THE, BY KATE MESSNER
(2009) FICTION [2]
AGE RANGE 8-12 / GRADE LEVEL 4-8 / 710L / THEME: BOTANY

Gianna Zales is not so crazy about research projects or anything involving time-management skills, and has somehow gotten to within a week of the due date of a huge science assignment with no work to show. But how hard can it be to find and catalog 25 different varieties of leaves—especially in Vermont. Winner of the 2010 E.B. White Read-Aloud medal for older readers.

NOTES: _____

CHARLOTTE'S WEB, BY E.B. WHITE (1952) FICTION [2]
AGE RANGE 8-12 / GRADE LEVEL 3-7 / 680L / THEME: NATURE

Charlotte's Web is a beloved children's classic and should be read by everyone from five to ninety-five. It is a story about wonderfully drawn characters including a little girl named Fern Arable who befriends a farm pig and names him Wilbur. When Wilbur is in danger of being slaughtered by the farmer his barn spider friend, Charlotte, writes messages praising Wilbur in her web in order to persuade the farmer to let him live. Winner of the 1953 Newbery Medal this is a beautifully written story about friendship. E. B. White also wrote *Stuart Little* and *The Trumpet of the Swan*.

NOTES: _____

CLOCKWORK OR ALL WOUND UP, BY PHILIP PULLMAN (1996)
FANTASY FICTION [2]
AGE RANGE 9-11 YEARS / GRADE LEVEL 3 AND UP / THEME: PHYSICS, MECHANICS

A spooky fantasy set in the town of Glockenheim in Germany in "the old days". The plot is exciting, suspenseful, and written in an ironic and amusing style. It has a strong moral message. Pullman said his novel was inspired by an old clock he came across in London's Science Museum. Noting the movement of the clock's gears, he wrote the story with elements that move in opposite directions. *Clockwork* has twice been adapted into an opera for children, adapted it into a shadow-play for adults and children, and into a stage play by Mutabilitie Productions.

NOTES: _____

COUNTDOWN CONSPIRACY, THE, BY KATIE SLIVENSKY (2017)
SCIENCE FICTION [2]
AGE RANGE 8-12 YEARS / GRADE LEVEL 3–7 / 700L / THEME: SPACE
TRAVEL

An adventure story set in the future with plenty of science action. Miranda Regent can't believe she was just chosen as one of six kids from around the world to train for the first ever mission to Mars. But as soon as the official announcement is made she begins receiving anonymous threatening messages. When the training base is attacked it looks like Miranda is the intended target. Now the entire mission—and everyone's lives—are at risk. And Miranda may be the only one who can save them.

NOTES: _____

DINOSAUR HUNTERS, BY CATHERINE CHAMBERS (2014)
FICTION [2}
AGE RANGE 8-10 / GRADE LEVEL 3–5 / THEME: ADVENTURE, TIME
TRAVEL, DINOSAURS

Three children, members of an unusual history club called SLIP (Secretly Living In the Past), have invented a time travel cell-phone app that enables them to physically travel back in time. In this adventure they encounter dinosaur hunters in Wyoming in the 1880's and become involved in a rivalry between two big-name fossil hunters.

A fun story with interesting and accurate historical and archeological information.

NOTES: _____

DINOSAURS BEFORE DARK, BY MARY POPE OSBORNE (1992)
FICTION [2]
AGE RANGE 6-9 / GRADE LEVEL 1–3 / 240L / ADVENTURE, TIME
TRAVEL, DINOSAURS

This is a Magic Tree House, No. 1 time-travel fantasy in which Jack and his younger sister find a tree house filled with books. When Jack wishes he could really see the Pteranodon pictured in one of them, it appears at the window. The children have been transported back to the Cretaceous period. Readers just past the easy-to-read stage will find it satisfying. Osborne has written 28 books in the The Magic Tree House series. Another series follows. As of January 2018 there are also 38 Magic Tree House Fact Trackers that are nonfiction companions to the fiction books. They provide more in-depth follow-up information on the topics in the series than already covered.

NOTES: _____

EARTH DRAGON AWAKES, THE: THE SAN FRANCISCO EARTHQUAKE OF 1906, BY LAURENCE YEP (2006) FACT BASED FICTION [2]
AGE RANGE 8-12 / GRADE LEVEL 3-7 / 510L / THEME: EARTH SCIENCE, LIVING THROUGH AN EARTHQUAKE

Based on actual events of the 1906 San Francisco earthquake and told from the perspectives of two young San Francisco friends, The Earth Dragon Awakes chronicles the story of the destruction of a city with realism and figurative language. This slim volume is beautifully written and an engaging read. Laurence Yep is the acclaimed author of more than sixty books for young people and a winner of the Laura Ingalls Wilder Award, and Newbery Honor Award.

NOTES: _____

ESCAPE FROM MR. LEMONCELLO'S LIBRARY, BY CHRIS GRABENSTEIN (2013) FICTION [2]
AGE RANGE: 8 - 12 / GRADE LEVEL: 3 – 7 / 720L / THEME: PROBLEM SOLVING

Twelve-year-old Kyle Keeley wins a coveted spot as one of twelve kids invited for an overnight sleepover in a new, futuristic library. The event is hosted by the famous game-maker Mr. Luigi Lemoncello and the kids get to enjoy lots of game-board games, word games and particularly video games. However, when morning comes the library doors stay locked and Kyle and the other kids must figure out clues and puzzles to find the hidden escape route. Cooperation and teamwork are encouraged. (An Agatha Award Winner and An ALA Notable Book)

The author, Chris Grabenstein, says that the book contains a secret puzzle for readers to decode. Two sequels to this tale are *Mr. Lemoncello's Library Olympics*, and *Mr. Lemoncello's Great Library Race*.

NOTES: _____

FEATHER CHASE, THE, BY SHANNON L. BROWN (2014)
FICTION [2]
AGE RANGE 8–12 / GRADE LEVEL: 3–6 / THEME: DETECTION, MYSTERY ADVENTURE

The Feather Chase is the first book (of three) in the Crime-Solving Cousins Mysteries. Science is used to help solve the mystery. The mystery concerns a case full of feathers. Great for the eight- to twelve-year-olds who enjoy Nancy Drew, or the Hardy Boys.
NOTES: _____

FIREWORK MAKER'S DAUGHTER, THE, BY PHILIP PULLMAN
(1995) FANTASY FICTION [2]
AGE RANGE 9-11 YEARS / GRADE LEVEL 3 AND UP / THEME: CHEMISTRY, FIRE, LIGHT

A magical adventure story, with a lot of incidental science content, in which a young girl called Lila wants to become a firework-maker, like her father, Lalchand. Despite Lila's talents, Lalchand believes this is an unsuitable job for girls. Lila disagrees, and embarks on a dangerous journey to get Royal Sulphur from Razvani the Fire-Fiend. To be successful Lila needs three gifts, talent, perseverance and luck. The story demonstrates whether or not she has these.
NOTES: _____

FRANKIE FILES, THE, BY A. J. PONDER (2017) FICTION [2]
AGE RANGE 8-12 /GRADE LEVEL 3-7 / THEME: INVENTION

Twelve-year-old Frankie Stein wants to be an inventor, but her inventions always get her into trouble. She started inventing at the age of 5 and the book describes those early inventions and the succeeding ones as she matures in years and experience to the age of 12. The novel is created from 14 interlocking short stories and 14 Invention Logbook entries. A mixture of science and make-believe this lighthearted book is perfect for young, fun loving, aspiring inventors, scientists and dreamers. Ponder is a New Zealand author and some of her books are published with NZ or British spelling.
NOTES: _____

GALILEO'S JOURNAL: 1609–1610, BY JEANNE PETTENATI
(2006) FICTION [2]
AGE RANGE 7-10 / GRADE LEVEL 2-4 / 660L / THEME: ASTRONOMY

Pettenati's fictional journal illustrates for the reader some of Galileo's curiosity and wonder as he makes some of the most amazing astronomical discoveries in history. The story focuses on his improvement of the telescope and his realization that planets other than the Earth also have moons and rotate around the sun rather than the Earth. The science and biographical information make this a brief but well-rounded look at the life's work of this famous Italian.

NOTES: _____

GEORGE'S SECRET KEY TO THE UNIVERSE, BY STEPHEN
HAWKING AND LUCY HAWKING (2007) FICTION [2]
AGE RANGE 9-11 / GRADE LEVEL 3-6 / 850L / THEME: ASTRONOMY

When George's pet pig breaks through the fence into the garden next door, George meets his new neighbors - Annie and her scientist father, Eric - and discovers a secret key that opens up a whole new way of looking at the world. From outer space!

This is the first in the smash-hit George series written by Lucy Hawking and her father, Professor Stephen Hawking. Space adventures and real-life information from the world's leading scientists—including Professor Hawking himself—make this a great book for curious kids. There are four sequels, *George's Cosmic Treasure Hunt* (2009), *George and the Big Bang* (2001), *George and the Unbreakable Code* (2014), and *George and the Blue Moon* (2016). The books are popular but have mixed reviews with some criticism of the stories but with praise for the presentation of the science aspects.

Lucy Hawking is the original creator of the George series. She works with world leading scientists, including her co-author and father, Stephen Hawking, to explain complex concepts of science through story telling to young readers.

NOTES: _____

GIRLS WHO LOOKED UNDER ROCKS, BY JEANINE ATKINS
(2000) NONFICTION [2]
AGE RANGE 10-16 YEARS / GRADE LEVEL 5-6 / 990L / THEME:
SCIENCE CAREERS

Stories of the lives of six pioneering naturalists portraying the youths
and careers of remarkable women whose curiosity about nature
fueled a passion to steadfastly overcome obstacles to careers in
traditionally men-only occupations. The six—Maria Merian (b.1647),
Anna Comstock (b.1854), Frances Hamerstrom (b.1907), Rachel
Carson (b.1907), Miriam Rothschild (b.1908), and Jane Goodall
(b.1934)—all became renowned scientists, artists and writers.
NOTES: _____

ITCH, BY SIMON MAYO (2012) FICTION [2]
AGE RANGE 9-11 / GRADE LEVEL 3-6 / THEME: CHEMISTRY, ELEMENTS

This book introduces changes of state to children. The story centers
on Itchingham Lofte, an element hunter who collects all the elements in the periodic table. Itch finds some are easy to get hold of
(chlorine in household bleach, his brother's titanium tongue stud),
but others are much harder to find. He acquires a brand new element, which puts him in great danger. Lots of people want to get
their hands on it. This makes for a thrilling action packed adventure
story. Itch uses his knowledge of chemistry to help him on his adventure and provides a setting in which children can explore: investigating dissolving, mixing and changes of state, and identifying and
comparing reversible and irreversible changes. Also by Simon Mayo:
Itch Rocks, and *Itchcraft*.
NOTES: _____

LONGLEAF, BY ROGER REID (2006) FICTION [2]
AGE RANGE 9 AND UP / GRADE LEVEL 4-6 / THEME: NATURE

When fourteen-year-old Jason accompanies his scientist parents on
a trip to the Conecuh National Forest in Alabama, he witnesses a
crime being committed and finds his own life endangered as a result.
Laced throughout are bits of environmental information about birds,
amphibians and the trees themselves. Readers learn about the
Longleaf Pine, prescribed fire, red-cockaded woodpeckers, gopher
tortoises, and many other components of this beautiful forest.
NOTES: _____

MATILDA, BY ROALD DAHL (1988) FICTION [2]
AGE RANGE 9-12 / GRADE LEVEL 3-6. / 840L / THEME: LOVE OF
LEARNING, SOME MATH CONCEPTS

Matilda is a little girl who, at age five-and-a-half, is doing double-digit multiplication problems and reading Dickens. Remarkably, her classmates love her even though she's a super-nerd and the teacher's pet. For a short period Matilda finds herself capable of telekinesis. Some science and math (fractions) concepts are implied in this book but little overt science information. *Matilda* won the Children's Book Award in 1999.

NOTES: _____

NEFERTITI, THE SPIDERNAUT: THE JUMPING SPIDER WHO LEARNED TO HUNT IN SPACE, BY DARCY PATTERSON (2016) NONFICTION [2]
AGE RANGE 7-10 / GRADE LEVEL 3-6 / THEME: EXPERIMENT, JUMPING SPIDER, SPACE

Nefertiti, the Spidernaut is the true story of a jumping spider sent to the International Space Station in 2012 to participate in an experiment, proposed by 18-year-old Amr Mohamed of Egypt. The question posed by the experiment was whether or not a jumping spider would be able to catch its food in space, and thus be able to survive. Nefertiti clocked a record-breaking 100 days in space, during which time she circled Earth about 1584 times, traveling about 41,580,000 miles. In spite of being weightless and isolated, Nefertiti adapted and learned to hunt. Against all odds, she survived to return to Earth, where she had to re-adapt to Earth's gravity. (Note: The reading category level is based more on the vocabulary than the visual presentation.)

NOTES: _____

ONE AND ONLY IVAN, THE, BY KATHERINE APPLEGATE (2012) FICTION [2]
AGE RANGE 8-12 YEARS / GRADE LEVEL 3-7 / 570L / THEME: FICTIONALIZED TRUE STORY, GORILLAS

This stirring novel from Katherine Applegate was inspired by the true story of a captive gorilla known as Ivan, this illustrated, first-person narration novel is told from the point-of-view of Ivan himself.

Having spent 27 years behind the glass walls of his enclosure in a shopping mall, Ivan has grown accustomed to humans watching him. He hardly ever thinks about his life in the jungle.

The One and Only Ivan was winner of the Newbery Medal. An author's note depicts the differences between the fictional story and true events.

NOTES: _____

RARE TREASURE: MARY ANNING AND HER REMARKABLE DISCOVERIES, BY DON BROWN (1999) FICTIONALIZED FACT [2]
AGE RANGE 6-9 / GRADE LEVEL 3-6 / 840L / THEME: DISCOVERY, FOSSILS, BIOGRAPHY

Over two hundred years ago, an eleven year-old girl discovered a fossil, and began a lifelong vocation that has earned her a place in history. Her story is one for dinosaur-lovers and for those who appreciate stories of strong girls. This is an easy-reading, slim book with interesting details about the life of Mary Anning and her real-life discovery of the first complete ichthyosaur fossil in southern England. She continued her avocation into adulthood and, despite being a self-taught archeologist, her contributions continue to inform the scientific community.

NOTES: _____

RIPTIDE, BY FRANCES WARD WELLER (1996) FACT-BASED FICTION [2]
AGE RANGE 5-8 / GRADE LEVEL: K-3 / 650L / THEME: ANIMAL, DOG, OCEAN

Zach's dog is no ordinary dog. He's strong, energetic, and loves the ocean. He lives up to his name, Riptide. He's a year-round beach bum, and a nuisance to all but Zach—until he saves the life of a little girl who's caught in a real riptide. This is a good, solid story, with terse, rhythmic writing. Robert Blake's oil paintings are wonderful in their engaging views of the ocean and beaches and countryside of Cape Cod. An adventure story starring a memorable canine character who's neither sentimentalized nor anthropomorphized. A good read-aloud book.

NOTES: _____

SCARECROW AND HIS SERVANT, THE, BY PHILIP PULLMAN
(2004) FAIRY TALE FICTION [2]
AGE RANGE 8-11 / GRADE LEVEL 3 AND UP / 850L / THEME: FANTASY

Old Mr. Pandolfo decides the time has come to create a scarecrow. Run-ins with government officials, soldiers, and unscrupulous business people provide plenty of opportunities for moralizing on the evils of society. Scarecrow's raison d'etre is to rescue his polluted valley from an evil ruling family. Described as having a 'touch of Dr. Doolittle', 'great charm and wit' and Shortlisted for the 2004 Carnegie Medal.

NOTES: _____

SILVERWING, BY KENNETH OPPEL (1997) FICTION [2]
AGE RANGE 8-12 YEARS / GRADE LEVEL 3-6 / 660L / THEME: BATS

Shade is a young Silverwing bat, the runt of his colony. But he's determined to prove himself on the long, dangerous winter migration to Hibernaculum, millions of wingbeats to the south. During a fierce storm, he loses the others and soon faces the most incredible journey of his young life. Kenneth Oppel had his first book published when he was 18. *Silverwing*, the first volume in a thrilling adventure trilogy set in the nocturnal world of bats, immediately captured the attention of middle readers.

NOTES: _____

STUART LITTLE, BY E.B. WHITE (1954) FICTION [2]
AGE RANGE 8-12 / GRADE LEVEL 3-7 / 500L / THEME: NATURE, MOUSE

Endearing for young and old, full of wit and wisdom and amusement. Engaging and clearly written before everything got either dumbed down or geared toward a reading level. A story highly enjoyable for kids and adults. Stuart Little is no ordinary mouse. Born to a family of humans, he lives in New York City with his parents, his older brother George, and Snowbell the cat. Though he's shy and thoughtful, he's also a true lover of adventure. Stuart's greatest adventure comes when his best friend, a beautiful little bird named Margalo, disappears from her nest.

NOTES: _____

SUMMER OF THE MONKEYS, BY WILSON RAWLS (1976)
FICTION [2]
AGE RANGE 8-12 / GRADE LEVEL 3-7 / 810L / THEME: ANIMAL BEHAVIOR

The story is set at the end of the nineteenth century and is about a 14-year-old boy who moves with his family to Oklahoma and discovers, in a nearby river bottom, monkeys that have escaped from a circus. He intends to return them to the circus and makes multiple attempts to capture them using traps and a net borrowed from his grandfather, but he gains only scratches and bites. From the author of the classic, *Where the Red Fern Grows*.
NOTES: _____

SWALLOWS AND AMAZONS, BY ARTHUR RANSOME (1930)
FICTION [2]
AGE RANGE 9 AND UP / GRADE LEVEL 3-6 / 800L / THEME: YOUTHFUL ADVENTURE, SAILING, WILDLIFE

There are 12 books in this series published between 1930 and 1947. Despite their age the stories are still wonderfully engaging for both the intended 9-12 year-old age group and older children – even adults. Very well written and (in modern editions) with delicate illustrative drawings by Ransome himself, they follow the summer adventures of several families of children who play and have real adventures together in their small sailing boats on the U.K. Norfolk Broads and in other locations too. The children have considerable freedom as was common in those days and many of their escapades involve the local wildlife. Birds are a pervasive theme especially in volume five, Coot Club, in which two of the main characters of the series become past of a club to protect local birds, their eggs and nests.
NOTES: _____

TIME, BY ROGER REID (2011) FICTION [2]
AGE RANGE 8-12 YEARS / GRADE LEVEL 3–6 / THEME: GEOLOGY, PALEONTOLOGY, MYSTERY

Set at the Steven C. Minkin Paleozoic Footprint Site near Birmingham in north Alabama, the richest source of vertebrate tracks of its age in the world, fourteen-year-old Jason and his friend Leah uncover a fossil thief and find an old enemy hunting them. Time is a fast-moving story that incorporates factual information about geology and paleontology into its intriguing tale of suspicion and pursuit. This is a witty and educational book and should intrigue middle-school readers.

NOTES: _____

TIN SNAIL, THE, BY CAMERON MCALLISTER (2014) FICTION [2]
AGE RANGE 9-12 / GRADE LEVEL 4-7 / 830L / THEME: INVENTION, MECHANICS, CARS

This book is based on the true story of the Citroen 2CV (the Deux Chevaux) car that was made in secret before the Second World War, and then became successful after the war. While living in Paris twelve year-old Angelo gives his father, a car engineer, an idea for a new aerodynamic car design. Later, living in a French village, Angelo persuades his dad to make an inexpensive car that can travel over bumpy ground with a special suspension so that local farmers who are too poor to buy the expensive cars that are for sale can get their produce safely to market over bumpy roads and in all weather. Well-plotted, great characters and plenty of humor.

NOTES: _____

TOM'S MIDNIGHT GARDEN, BY PHILIPPA PEARCE (1958)
FANTASY FICTION [2]
AGE RANGE 8-12 / GRADE LEVEL 3-7 / 860L /THEME: TIME SLIP

This is a beautifully written, gentle, very engaging novel about a young boy named Tom, who slips into a different time period each time he visits a magical garden to meet a young girl named Hattie. For the purposes of this list a special aspect of the story is the development of the time slip aspect and a recognition of the fact that time behaves strangely and we don't entirely understand how it works except on a day-to-day level. (The story makes use of a theory of time from J.W. Dunne's 1927 nonfiction, adult book *An Experiment with Time*.) Pearce won the 1858 Carnegie Medal for the story. Her other books include *Minnow on the Say*.

NOTES: _____

TREASURE (SEED SAVERS BOOK 1), BY S. SMITH (2012) FICTION [2]
AGE RANGE 9-12 / GRADE LEVEL: 4-8 / 660L / THEME: SEEDS,
GARDENING

The year is 2077 and in twelve-year-old Clare's world, blueberry is just a flavor and apples are found only in fairy tales. There has been no apocalypse, but things like the weather, the Internet, and food are different. One day Clare meets a woman who teaches her about seeds and real food and Clare and her friends learn about gardening despite suspicions that it is illegal. When the authorities discover the children's forbidden tomato plant and arrest their mother, Clare and her brother embark upon lonely cross-country journey to find the place called the Garden State.

Treasure is book one of a four book series. The characters in each of the three subsequent books get progressively older. The author suggests that children start with book 1, *Treasure*. Teens, start with book 2, *Lily*. Adults, start with book 3, *Heirloom*.

NOTES: _____

TRICKING THE TALLYMAN, BY JACQUELINE DAVIES (2014)
FICTION [2]
AGE RANGE 5-8 YEARS / GRADE LEVEL KINDERGARTEN – 3 / 660L /
THEME: MATH, DATA TABULATION

One day in 1790, Phineus Bump rides into Tunbridge, VT. His job is to count every man, woman, and child in town and report back to the government. But folks are skeptical. Charming and humorous, this book is certain to appeal. *Tricking the Tallyman,* beautifully illustrated by S.D. Schindler, accomplishes the task of showing kids the way the 1790 census was tabulated (or tallied). It is a great example of how data tracking is used in real life. In this case the story has a historical context but the process is a vital part of science research and documentation too.

NOTES: _____

TRUMPET OF THE SWAN, THE, BY E.B. WHITE (1970)
FICTION [2]
AGE RANGE 8-12 / GRADE LEVEL 3-7 / 750L / THEME: PROBLEM
SOLVING

A delightful classic about overcoming obstacles, persistence, problem solving and the joy of music. Like the rest of his family, Louis is a trumpeter swan. But unlike his four brothers and sisters, Louis can't trumpet joyfully. In fact, he can't even make a sound. And since he can't trumpet his love, the beautiful swan Serena pays absolutely no attention to him. Louis tries everything he can think of to win Serena's affection—he even goes to school to learn to read and write. Then his father finds him a real trumpet. Is a musical instrument the key to winning Louis his love?

NOTES: _____

VINCENT SHADOW: TOY INVENTOR, BY TIM KEHOE (2009) FICTION [2]
AGE RANGE 8-12 / GRADE LEVEL 3-7 / 770L/ THEME: INVENTION

Tim Kehoe, a real-life toy inventor, wrote two books about eleven-year-old Vincent Shadow. *Vincent Shadow: Toy Inventor* was the first. Vincent's creative ideas come to him in the form of brilliant, fully formed, detailed visions and he likes to think that his ideas come to him in a way that is similar to those of the famous physicist Nikola Tesla. Vincent keeps his inventions secret from his family. His attic lab is crammed with toy prototypes and he has a sketch book filled with drawings of toys he still wants to build. His opportunity comes when he learns of a toy-invention contest with a prize that would help him continue inventing. (The sequel is called *Top Secret Toys*.)

NOTES: _____

WHEN YOU REACH ME, BY REBECCA STEAD (2009) FICTION [2]
AGE RANGE 9-12 / GRADE LEVEL 5-7 / 750L / THEME: SCIENCE FICTION

Sixth-grader Miranda lives in 1978 New York City with her mother, and her life compass is Madeleine L'Engle's *A Wrinkle in Time*. When she receives a series of enigmatic notes that claim to want to save her life, she comes to believe that they are from someone who knows the future. This Newbery Medal winner that has a fantastic puzzle at its heart has been called "smart and mesmerizing," (The New York Times), and "superb" (The Wall Street Journal). Winner of the Boston Globe–Horn Book Award for Fiction, A New York Times Bestseller and Notable Book.

NOTES: _____

WHO REALLY KILLED COCK ROBIN? AN ECOLOGICAL
MYSTERY, BY JEAN CRAIGHEAD GEORGE (1971) FICTION [2]
AGE RANGE 8-12 YEARS / GRADE LEVEL 3-7 / 830L / THEME:
ECOLOGY

The story involves the ins and outs of real life everyday ecology and
how all things are connected. It traces the impact of human activity
on the local environment of the fictional town discovering hidden
damage in many corners of the town from fertilizers, pesticides,
industrial toxins, and other pollutants. The task of the young investi-
gators is to try to track what effect these had on Cock Robin, his
mate, and their mostly-failed clutch of eggs.

NOTES: _____

WILD ROBOT, THE, BY PETER BROWN (2016) FICTION [2]
AGE RANGE 8-12 / GRADE LEVEL 3–6 / 740L / THEME: ROBOTS

Peter Brown, the author, says, " I loved imagining scenes of nature
living in surprising places and that got me thinking about scenes of
unnatural things living in surprising places." Can a robot survive in
the wilderness? When robot Roz opens her eyes for the first time,
she discovers that she is alone on a remote, wild island. She has no
idea how she got there or what her purpose is—but she knows she
needs to survive. She realizes she must adapt to her surroundings
and learn from the island's unwelcoming animal inhabitants. A fine,
engrossing story. Brown has written a sequel, *The Wild Robot Escapes*.

NOTES: _____

WILD WINGS, BY GILL LEWIS (2011) FICTION [2]
AGE RANGE 8-12 YEARS / GRADE LEVEL 3–6 / 600L / THEME:
ECOLOGY, OSPREY

A moving and inspirational story, based on valid osprey research,
about eleven-year-old Callum and his friend Iona from Scotland who
discover a pair of osprey with an aerie on Callum's farm. Jeneba, a
girl from West Africa, joins Callum to save the female that they have
named Iris, as she migrates to Africa and then back to Scotland. A
strong ecological theme runs through the novel, Striving to protect
the osprey nesting on his family's farm in Scotland, 11-year-old
Callum McGregor watches the bird throughout summer and uses a
computer to follow her migration to Africa. The book includes
weblinks to resources with webcam videos and information about

ongoing osprey research in Scotland and around the world.

NOTES: _____

WISDOM, THE MIDWAY ALBATROSS, BY DARCY PATTISON
(2012) NARRATIVE NONFICTION [2]
AGE RANGE 6-12 / GRADE LEVEL 3-5 / THEME: BIOLOGY, BIRDS,
ALBATROSS, RESEARCH

The author tells the true story of Wisdom, a female Laysan Albatross. The bird was first tagged by scientists in 1956 and is alive
today, having lived through multiple natural disasters, and man-
made threats. The albatross spends most of her time at sea and
discarded plastic and the 2011 Japanese earthquake and tsunami are
among the hazards she has escaped. The USGS has tracked Wisdom
since she was tagged, and has logged that she has flown over three
million miles since 1956. Pattison has included closing notes that
provide information and resources for an interested reader.

NOTES: _____

WONDERFUL FLIGHT TO THE MUSHROOM PLANET, THE,
BY ELEANOR CAMERON (1954) FICTION [2]
AGE RANGE 8-11 / GRADE LEVEL 3-6 / 970L / THEME: SCIENCE
FICTION, SPACE TRAVEL

This is a classic science fiction fantasy, about two boys and their
space ship, and adventures on a planet found not far away from
Earth. Basidium-X, the Mushroom Planet, exists only in the world of
imagination. The science is well researched. (Book 1 of 5)

NOTES: _____

*"Fools have a habit of believing that
everything written by a famous author
is admirable. For my part I read
only to please myself and like only what
suits my taste."*

—VOLTAIRE, CANDID

Proficient Reader Stories

ADMIRAL RICHARD BYRD: ALONE IN THE ANTARCTIC, BY PAUL RINK (2005) BIOGRAPHY [3]
AGE RANGE 12 AND UP / GRADE LEVEL 6-8 / 960L / THEME: EXPLORATION, SURVIVAL

This is the story of Richard Byrd as he survives for six months in -60F temperatures in his bid to explore The South Pole. This biography chronicles Byrd's 1934 journey into the frozen south, and his bid to survive the harsh Antarctic landscape. During his voyage, Byrd became hopelessly lost in the frozen tundra. Byrd's story is a tale of personal courage and dedication, all set against a backdrop of perhaps the harshest environment on earth.

NOTES: _____

BEYOND THE BRIGHT SEA, BY LAUREN WOLK (2017)
FICTION [3]
AGE RANGE 10-14 / GRADE LEVEL 5-7 / 770L / THEME: MYSTERY, SUSPENSE, NATURAL HISTORY.

The story of an orphan girl trying to discover who she is and who she wants to be. It's the 1920s, Crow and her adoptive father, Osh, live on a tiny island off Cape Cod. Excellent writing and plot development skillfully blend shipwrecks, leprosy, and a seaside landscape with the terror the ocean can unleash as a furious nor'easter heightens tension later in the book.

An NPR Best Book of the Year • A Parents' Magazine Best Book of the Year • A HornBook Fanfare Selection • A Kirkus Best Book of the Year • A School Library Journal Best Book of the Year • A Southern Living Best Book of the Year • A New York Public Library Best Book of the Year

NOTES: _____

BOOK SCAVENGER, THE, BY JENNIFER CHAMBLISS BERTMAN
(2015) FICTION [3]
AGE RANGE 9–14 / GRADE LEVEL 4–6. THEME: MYSTERY, PROBLEM
SOLVING, ADVENTURE,

San Francisco landmarks and their rich literary histories lead two friends on a quest to solve clues left behind in an Edgar Allan Poe book by publisher and Book Scavenger mastermind Garrison Griswold. When 12-year-old Emily Crane, a book enthusiast and puzzle-solver, moves into her new apartment, she meets James Lee, a cipher-solving whiz with a cowlick he's named Steve. The story reinforces the value of intellectual curiosity, reading, problem-solving, history, adventure, and being open to new experiences. Puzzling out the clever ciphers fascinates and adds dimension and curiosity to each quest. There are several sequels including *The Unbreakable Code*.
NOTES: _____

BORN FREE, BY JOY ADAMSON (1960) TRUE STORY, PERSONAL
NARRATIVE [3]
AGE RANGE 12 AND UP / GRADE LEVEL 6-10 / THEME: ANIMAL
BEHAVIOR, LIONS

The story of Elsa the lioness cub introduces young people to the wildlife of Africa with a lively story and very appealing photographs. Elsa lived for a while with Joy Adamson and her husband in their home in Kenya but they wanted her to be free and so they spent many months training her to hunt and survive on her own. Which she did. Adamson wrote two sequels, *Living Free*, and *Forever Free*.
NOTES: _____

CASE OF THE MISSING MOONSTONE, THE, THE
WOLLSTONECRAFT DETECTIVE AGENCY, BOOK 1 BY JORDAN
STRATFORD (2015)
FICTION [3]
AGE RANGE 8-12 / GRADE LEVEL 4-7 / THEME: DETECTIVE MYSTERY

History, mystery, and science collide in this series. In Book 1 Jordan Stratford imagines an alternate 1826 in which he adjusts the histori-cal timeline to fit the story. The protagonists are two historically real girls whose ages have been changed to make them three years apart in age rather than eighteen. In this tale Ada Byron Lovelace (now known as the world's first computer programmer) is 11 and

Mary Godwin Shelley (author of Frankenstein) is 14. They form a secret detective agency. Ada has a mathematical frame of mind and great curiosity. Mary earned her university degree in science and literature. She wrote over 100 books most of which should probably be mentioned here but this list is limiting their inclusion to five.

NOTES: _____

CHASING VERMEER, BY BLUE BALLIETT (2004) FICTION [3]
AGE RANGE 9-12 YEARS / GRADE LEVEL 4–7 / 770L / THEME: ART MYSTERY

The story is set in Hyde Park, Chicago. When a book and a letter bring two sixth grade children, Calder Pillay and Petra Andalee, together, strange things start to happen and an invaluable Vermeer painting disappears. Calder enjoys puzzles and Pentominoes. Petra wants to be a writer. The two find themselves drawn clue by clue into an international art scandal. They must draw on their powers of intuition, their problem solving skills, and their knowledge of Vermeer to solve the mystery. There is a code, involving Pentominoes and frogs, hidden in the illustrations throughout the book. The story has been called "a puzzle, wrapped in a mystery, disguised as an adventure, and delivered as a work of art." It is a winner of the Edgar and Agatha awards.

NOTES: _____

DRAGON BONES AND DINOSAUR EGGS, BY ANN BAUSUM (2000) TRUE STORY [3]
AGE RANGE 11-14 / GRADE LEVEL 5-8 / 1080L / THEME: PALEONTOLOGY, DINOSAURS, EXPLORATION

This slim, well-researched book is a record of the accomplishments of explorer Roy Chapman Andrews with quotes from his writings and personal letters, and with fine sepia-toned photographs. Andrew's adventurous spirit and organizational skills opened a new age in scientific exploration, using then-modern technology and a diverse team of experts in various fields. Over a 12 year period, he conducted several intensive expeditions into Mongolia and central Asia, uncovering the first dinosaur eggs and the first fossils of Protoceratops, Oviraptor, and Velociraptor.

NOTES: _____

EVERY LIVING THING: THE WARM AND JOYFUL MEMOIRS OF THE WORLD'S MOST BELOVED ANIMAL DOCTOR, BY JAMES HERRIOT (1992) FACT BASED FICTION [3]
AGE RANGE AN ADULT BOOK ENJOYED BY READERS AGED 12 AND UP / THEME: A VETERINARIAN'S LIFE WORK

For decades, Herriot roamed the remote, beautiful Yorkshire Dales, treating every patient that came his way from smallest to largest, and observing animals and humans alike with his keen, loving eye. Throughout, Herriot's deep compassion, humor, and love of life shine out as readers laugh, cry, and delight in his portraits of his many, varied animal patients and their equally varied owners. This is number 6 in a series that has been made into a very popular TV series titled "All Things Bright and Beautiful."

NOTES: _____

EVOLUTION OF CALPURNIA TATE, THE, BY JACQUELINE KELLY (2009) FICTION [3]
AGE RANGE 9-12 / GRADE LEVEL 5–8 / 830L / THEME: NATURE

Calpurnia Virginia Tate, (Callie), is eleven years old in 1899 living in a small Texas town. She surprises her grandfather when she tells him that she wonders why the yellow grasshoppers in her Texas backyard are so much bigger than the green ones. This is the start of a companionship in which Callie becomes most content when observing and collecting scientific specimens with her grandfather. Interwoven with the scientific theme are threads of daily life in a large family at the turn of the century. (Sequel, *The Curious World of Calpurnia Tate*). Book 1 of 2 in the Calpurnia Tate Series. A 2010 Newbery Honor Book.

NOTES: _____

EYE OF THE STORM, BY KATE MESSNER (2012) FICTION [3]
AGE RANGE 10-14 / GRADE LEVEL: 4-7 / 740L / THEME: METEOROLOGY

A suspenseful science thriller. In the story's not-too-distant future, huge tornadoes and monster storms are a part of everyday life. Jaden Meggs attends a summer science camp, Eye on Tomorrow, that her dad founded. There she meets Alex, a boy from a nearby storm-ravaged farm, and they learn a horrible truth about Jaden's dad's weather research. As a massive tornado approaches, Jaden must trust her knowledge and have faith in herself to confront her dad and save everyone from the biggest storm yet.

Also by Kate Messner are books at many levels including: *Over and Under the Snow*. [1]

NOTES: _____

FINDING THE LONE WOMAN OF SAN NICOLAS ISLAND,
BY R.C. NIDEVER (2017) NONFICTION NOVEL [3]
AGE RANGE 13 AND UP / GRADE LEVEL 7 AND UP / THEME: SURVIVAL, ANTHROPOLOGY.

Based on the same story as *Island of the Blue Dolphins*, Nidever's novel is told much more completely and from a different perspective. R.C. Nidever's novel is based on the true story of a California Indian woman left alone on a remote island in the year 1835 and the man, George Nidever, who finally found her. While some of its characters and events are fictional, R.C. Nidever's book draws heavily on the recollections of his ancestor George Nidever, and of Carl Dittman who was the first person to find the Lone Woman on San Nicolas Island in 1853.

NOTES: _____

FOURTEENTH GOLDFISH, THE, BY JENNIFER L. HOLM (2014)
FICTION [3]
AGE RANGE 10-13 / GRADE LEVEL 5-7 / 550L / THEME: SCIENCE DISCOVERY

Eleven-year-old Ellie Cruz's life changes dramatically when her mother brings a teenage boy home one night and she learns it is her estranged grandfather, Melvin. Melvin is a scientist who has figured out how to reverse aging and is now 13 again. Ellie's interest in science blossoms, and she is eager to help Melvin retrieve a jellyfish specimen he used in his experiments so he can publish his discovery about eternal youth. Ellie learns about the work of Jonas Salk, Robert Oppenheimer, and Marie Curie. As she learns more, she realizes that scientific discoveries often have unforeseen consequences. Holm is a Newbery Medal winning author of *When You Reach Me*, included in this list.

NOTES: _____

FUZZY MUD, BY LOUIS SACHAR (2015) FICTION [3]
AGE RANGE 10 AND UP / GRADE LEVEL 4-8 / 700L / THEME: ENVIRONMENT AND CHEMISTRY

Newbery Award-winning author Sachar takes on science and the government in this engaging eco-cautionary tale. Middle schoolers Tamaya, Marshall, and Chad meet in the woods near their school. When Tamaya stops the boys' fighting by throwing some strange-looking mud in Chad's face an environmental disaster is inadvertently unleashed. The mud has been created by a nearby research facility. Clever petri dish design elements and multiplication equations sprinkled throughout the text help readers grasp the simple math that challenges science's claims of control.

NOTES: _____

GEBRA NAMED AL, A, BY WENDY ISDELL (1993) FANTASY FICTION [3]
AGE RANGE 11-14 / GRADE LEVEL 5-8 / THEME: MATHEMATICS, CHEMISTRY

Julie hates algebra until she journeys to the fantastical Land of Mathematics, where she encounters a zebra like imaginary number named Al and several horse like creatures representing the elements of the periodic table. Winner of multiple awards for educational fiction as well as quality fantasy.

NOTES: _____

GREAT TROUBLE, THE: A MYSTERY OF LONDON, THE BLUE DEATH, AND A BOY CALLED EEL, BY DEBORAH HOPKINSON (2013) NARRATIVE NONFICTION NOVEL [3]
AGE RANGE 10 AND UP / GRADE LEVEL 5-7 / 660L / THEME: MEDICAL MYSTERY, PUBLIC HEALTH, MICROBIOLOGY,

Eel, a twelve-year-old orphan and a London "mudlark," spends his days in the filthy River Thames, searching for bits of things to sell. Eel has a secret that costs him four shillings a week to keep safe. But things aren't that bad until an August day in 1854—the day the deadly cholera ("blue death") comes to Broad Street. Everyone believes that cholera is spread through poisonous air. But one man, Dr. John Snow, has a different theory. As the epidemic progresses, it's up to Eel and his best friend, Florrie, to help gather evidence to prove Dr. Snow's theory—before the entire neighborhood is wiped out. The story has historical accuracy, scientific inquiry, and medical informa-tion presented in an engaging, and easy-to-understand way.

For adults and older readers the story of this cholera epidemic is very well told by Steven Johnson in *The Ghost Map* published in 2006.

NOTES: _____

HATCHET, BY GARY PAULSEN (1987) FICTION SURVIVAL STORY [3] AGE RANGE 12-14 / GRADE LEVEL 6-8 / 1020L / THEME: WILDERNESS SURVIVAL.

Thirteen-year-old Brian Robeson is on his way to visit his father when the single-engine plane in which he is flying crashes. Suddenly, Brian finds himself alone in the Canadian wilderness with nothing but a tattered Windbreaker and the hatchet his mother gave him as a present. Brian has no time for anger, self-pity, or despair—it will take all his know-how and determination, and more courage than he knew he possessed, to survive. This is book one of five in a series in which Brian grows up to have more adventures. Winner of the Newbery Honor.

NOTES: _____

HOOT, BY CARL HIASSEN (2002) FICTION [3] AGE RANGE 10-15 / GRADE LEVEL 5-6 / 760L / THEME: ECOLOGY, OWLS

An ecological mystery, involving endangered miniature owls, a pancake house scheduled to be built over their burrows, and three middle school kids determined to beat the screwed-up adult system and save the owls. A 2003 Newbery Honor-winner.

(In Hiassen's 2012 Newbery Honor winner *Chomp*, his latest novel for ages 12-14 years, he takes on a wildlife reserve that cares for animals to be sold as pets or to perform in animal shows, and reality TV.)

NOTES: _____

HOUSE OF THE SCORPION, THE, BY NANCY FARMER (2002) FICTION [3] AGE RANGE 12 AND UP /GRADE LEVEL 7 AND UP / THEME: BIOTECHNOLOGY, CLONING

This story is set in the near future; a gripping, gritty science fiction, coming-of-age story in a country called Opium. Opium is a country of vast poppy fields lying between the United States and what was once called Mexico. The leading character, a boy called Matteo Alacrán, was not born he was cloned. His DNA came from El Patrón, lord of Opium. Life in Opium is not easy for Matteo and he is struggling to be free and to establish his own identity.

This is Book 1 in the Matteo Alacran Series and was the National Book Award Winner for Young People's Literature, the Newbery Honor Book, and the Printz Honor Book.

NOTES: _____

IN THE SHADOW OF MAN, BY JANE GOODALL (1971) TRUE STORY, PERSONAL NARRATIVE [3]
AGE RANGE 13 AND UP / GRADE LEVEL 8 AND UP / 1220L / THEME: PRIMATES/CHIMPANZEES

World-renowned primatologist, conservationist, and humanitarian Dr. Jane Goodall's account of her life among the wild chimpanzees is an enthralling story of animal behavior. *In the Shadow of Man* is an account of Goodall's early years at Africa's Gombe Stream Reserve, telling us of the remarkable discoveries she made as she got to know the chimps and they got to know her.

NOTES: _____

ISAAC THE ALCHEMIST: SECRETS OF ISAAC NEWTON, REVEAL'D, BY MARY LOSURE (2017) NARRATIVE NONFICTION [3]
AGE RANGE 10-13 / GRADE LEVEL 6-8 / 1010L / THEME: BIOGRAPHY, PHYSICS, ASTRONOMY

Mary Losure tells the story of Isaac Newton's early life growing up in an apothecary's house in a time before "science" as we know it today existed. Losure tells of his difficult and troubled childhood, his prodigious talent at Cambridge, his prickly and reclusive nature, and his famous Laws of Motion.

NOTES: _____

ISLAND OF THE BLUE DOLPHINS, BY SCOTT O'DELL (1960) NONFICTION NOVEL [3]
AGE RANGE 13 AND UP / GRADE LEVEL 7 AND UP, YOUNG ADULT FICTION / 1000L / THEME: NATURE, SURVIVAL

The story of Karana, a young Indian girl stranded alone for eighteen years on an island off the California coast. Blue dolphins swim around the island, otters, sea elephants, and sea birds abound. Once, Indians also lived on the island. When they all left one young girl was left behind. The book is based on the true story, *The Lone Woman of San Nicolas Island.*

Nearly 60 years later R.C. Nidever wrote the 2017 *Finding the Lone Woman of San Nicolas Island* that tells this story from the point of view of the people who were alive at the time, and details the times they lived in. While some of its characters and events are fictional, R.C. Nidever's book also draws heavily on the recollections of his ancestor George Nidever, and of Carl Dittman who was the first person to find the Lone Woman on San Nicolas Island in 1853. Nidever's book is included in this booklist.

NOTES: _____

ISLAND OF THE UNKNOWNS: A MYSTERY, BY BENEDICT CAREY (2011) FICTION [3]
AGE RANGE 8-13 / GRADE LEVEL 4-8 / 760L / THEME: MATHEMATICS, MYSTERY

A clever mystery story for young would-be mathematicians. On a circular island where the Folsom Nuclear Plant is located, two eleven year-old friends live in a trailer park called Folsom Adjacent. When people start vanishing from their trailer-park home, the two friends investigate, using mathematical cues left behind by their missing math tutor. Equations, right triangles, pi, coordinates, and slope help the kids negotiate a massive maze of underground tunnels and discover a nefarious scheme that could destroy the island. Math moves the plot along with diagrams, charts, and illustrated problems.

NOTES: _____

JACK AND THE GENIUSES – AT THE BOTTOM OF THE WORLD, BY BILL NYE AND GREGORY MONE (2017) FICTION [3]
AGE RANGE 8-13 / GRADE LEVEL 4-8 / 680L / THEMES: SCIENCE, SCIENCE DISCOVERIES, ADVENTURE AND HOMEMADE DRONES.

New York Times bestselling authors Bill Nye the Science Guy and Gregory Mone take middle-grade readers on a scientific adventure. The perfect combination to engage and entertain readers, the series features real-world science along with action and a mystery that will leave kids guessing until the end. In this first volume, *Jack and the*

Geniuses: At The Bottom of The World, readers meet Jack and his foster siblings, Ava and Matt, who are orphans. But they're not your typical kind of orphans—they're geniuses. Ava speaks multiple languages and builds robots for fun, and Matt is into astronomy and is a whiz at math. Further books so far in the Jack and the Geniuses series include *In the Deep Blue Sea* (2017), and *Lost In the Jungle* (2018).

NOTES: _____

JULIE OF THE WOLVES, BY JEAN CRAIGHEAD GEORGE (1972) FICTION [3]
AGE RANGE 9–13 / GRADE LEVEL 3-7 / THEME: ENVIRONMENT AND NATURAL WORLD, SURVIVAL IN THE WILD, WOLVES.

An Eskimo girl lost on the Alaskan tundra survives by copying the ways of a pack of wolves that befriends her. 1973 Newbery Award winner. (The Julie Trilogy includes *Julie of the Wolves* (1972), *Julie* (1994), and *Julie's Wolf Pack* (1997)).

Jean Craighead George was born into a family of naturalists and she earned her university degree in science and literature. She wrote over 100 books.

NOTES: _____

KINE, BY A. R. LLOYD (1982) FICTION [3]
AGE RANGE 11 UP / GRADE LEVEL 5 UP / THEME: NATURAL HISTORY, WOODLANDS, LEAST WEASELS.

The young least weasel Kine lives alone at the place of his birth in a valley beneath the roots of an old fallen willow dubbed the Life Tree. It is a peaceful valley of woodland, hedgerows and marsh, unchanged for centuries until a ferocious invader appears: wild mink, savage and unstoppable. It is left to a brave but tiny hunter, Kine the weasel, to fight back against the she-mink Gru and her dark followers. The animals are given semi anthropomorphic human characters. The author writes like a poet, a man with a love of nature who captures the passage of the seasons and the beauty of Britain's countryside in lyrical prose. However, there are some gruesome passages illustrating true life-facts of the riverbank life that could worry a younger child. The weasel, Mustela nivalis, is native to Eurasia, North America and North Africa.

NOTES: _____

LIFE ON SURTSEY: ICELAND'S UPSTART ISLAND, BY LOREE BURNS (2017) NARRATIVE NONFICTION [3]
AGE RANGE 11-14 YEARS & UP / GRADE LEVEL 7-9 / 1090L / THEME: GEOLOGY, BIOLOGY

This is a fascinating look at the birth and evolution of a volcanic island. But, more importantly, it's the story of entomologist Erling Ólafsson who is passionate about his work. Closely following a 5-day research trip to the island of Surtsey, the book focuses on what it's really like to be a scientist doing fieldwork. Author Loree Burns includes fascinating details such as the meticulous gathering of insects to the evening meals to where you go when you have to more-than-pee. Entertaining, informative, and inspiring! Very read-able by adults.

NOTES: _____

MARY ANDROMEDA AND THE AMAZING EYE, BY J.G. KEMP (2016) FICTION [3]
AGE RANGE 9-12 / GRADE LEVEL 4-8 / THEME: ASTRONOMY, MYSTERY

When 11-year-old Mary Andromeda is spirited away to Evergreen Isle, an abandoned island-of-science, she discovers things about her long-lost mother, the plans of a secret scientific society, and her own place in an ancient family of astronomers. The story is full of myster-ies to solve by using astronomy, computers, secret tunnels, hidden messages, and adventure. (This is the first in the Journals of Ever-green Isle books).

NOTES: _____

MISCALCULATIONS OF LIGHTNING GIRL, THE, BY STACY MCANUITY (2018) FICTION [3]
AGE RANGE 8-12 / GRADE LEVEL 4-7 / 530L / THEME: MATH

Lucy, the main character, is a mathematical genius. She was struck by lightning when she was 8 and when she woke up, she was a genius about all things math and number-related. Ever since the zap gave her genius-level math skills Lucy has been home schooled. Now, at 12 years old, she's technically ready for college. She just has to pass 1 more test—she has to spend a year in school in seventh grade, make 1 friend, join 1 activity, and read 1 book (that's not a math textbook!). With Lucy's fun, funny fascination with numbers, even the most mathematical-averse reader will come away from this book with a new appreciation for and understanding of complex numerical concepts (but they'll never suspect).

NOTES: _____

MRS. FRISBY AND THE RATS OF NIMH, BY ROBERT C.
O'BRIEN (1971) FICTION [3]
AGE RANGE 9-12 / GRADE LEVEL 4-6 / 790L / THEME: SCIENCE,

This is a fictional story of a mouse family and a society of NIMH rats (National Institute of Mental Health) rendered intelligent by scientific experimentation. Mrs. Frisby is a widowed mouse with four small children, and is faced with a terrible problem. She must move her family to their summer quarters immediately, or face almost certain death. But her youngest son, Timothy, lies ill with pneumonia and must not be moved. Luckily she meets up with some of the rats of NIMH who come up with a solution to her dilemma. Mrs. Frisby in turn renders them a service. A 1972 Newbery Medal award winner, this is book 1 of 3 in the NIMH Series

NOTES: _____

MY FAMILY AND OTHER ANIMALS, BY GERALD DURRELL
(1956) AUTOBIOGRAPHY [3]
AGE RANGE 10 UP / GRADE LEVEL 6 UP / THEME: PERSONAL
COLLECTION OF ANIMALS, CORFU,

This is an autobiographical account of five years in the childhood of naturalist Gerald Durrell when he moved with his family to live on the island of Corfu. With snakes in the bath and scorpions on the lunch table, the house is a bit like a zoo so they should feel right at home. Ten-year-old Gerald doesn't know why his older brothers and sisters complain so much. The author's brother, Lawrence Durrell, is quoted as saying, "This is a very wicked, very funny, and I'm afraid rather truthful book." Gerald Durrell was a naturalist, author, conservationist and a passionate and persuasive advocate of the need for the conservation of animals and plants and their habitats.

NOTES: _____

MY SEASON WITH PENGUINS: AN ANTARCTIC JOURNAL,

BY SOPHIE WEBB (2000) NARRATIVE NONFICTION [3]
AGE RANGE 10 AND UP / GRADE LEVEL 5-7 / 1040L / THEME:
BIOLOGY, BIRDS, PENGUINS, RESEARCH

Through an effective blend of journal entries and illustrations the author presents a great deal of science information about the penguins as well as the difficulties of working in the cold Antarctic environment. Webb explicitly states the questions to be studied by the scientists on the expedition and shows the scientific method in action. The research takes place at the U.S. base, McMurdo, on Ross Island. The subjects of the research are "fearless, round-bellied, pink-footed, gliding, diving, utterly adept Adélie penguins."

NOTES: _____

MY SIDE OF THE MOUNTAIN, BY JEAN CRAIGHEAD GEORGE

(1959) FICTION [3]
AGE RANGE 13 AND UP / GRADE LEVEL 7 AND UP / YOUNG ADULT
FICTION / THEME: NATURE

An adventure novel featuring a boy who learns about courage, independence, and the need for companionship while attempting to live alone in a forested area of New York state. It has received several honors: the Newbery Award Honors list, American Library Association's Notable Book list for 1959, the Hans Christian Anderson Award 1959 honors list, a 1965 Lewis Carroll Shelf Award citation, and the 1959 George G. Stone Center for Children's Books Award. Book critic Eden Ross Lipson noted that it "skillfully blends themes of nature, courage, curiosity, and independence". By 1998, the book had been translated into numerous foreign languages.

Jean Craighead George was born into a family of naturalists and she earned her university degree in science and literature. She wrote over 100 books.

NOTES: _____

MY SISTER ROSALIND FRANKLIN: A FAMILY MEMOIR, BY

JENIFER GLYNN (2012) BIOGRAPHY [3]
AGE RANGE THIS IS AN ADULT BOOK READABLE BY GOOD READERS
OF 12 AND UP / THEME: BIOGRAPHY, BIOTECHNOLOGY, DISCOVERY
OF DNA

Rosalind Franklin is famous in the history of science for her contribution to the discovery of the structure of DNA. Much has been written about the importance of her part, and about how her work was affected by her position as a woman scientist. In this family memoir her sister, the writer and historian Jenifer Glynn, paints a picture of Rosalind's background, early education, time as a science student at Cambridge, to her life as an adult. Glynn shows how much her sister achieved and how she was influenced by the social and intellectual climate of the period when she worked.

(Also listed in this bibliography is *The Annotated and Illustrated Double Helix,* by James D. Watson.)

NOTES: _____

MYSTERIOUS BENEDICT SOCIETY, THE, BY TRENTON LEE STEWART (2017) FICTION [3]
AGE RANGE 9–13 / GRADE LEVEL 4-7 / 890L / THEME: MYSTERY, PROBLEM SOLVING, ADVENTURE

The story follows the adventures of four eleven to twelve year old children: Reyne Muldoon, George "Sticky" Washington, Kate Wetherall, and Constance Contraire, who respond to an add in the newspaper that says, "Are you a gifted child looking for special opportunities?" The four children create the Mysterious Benedict Society, named after the eccentric Mr. Benedict who is responsible for gathering them together in this, the first book of a trilogy. Their challenge is to go undercover at the Learning Institute for the Very Enlightened on a secret mission that 'only the most intelligent and inventive children can accomplish'. The task is to investigate a mysterious threat plaguing the world in the form of secret messages transmitted into people's minds via television and radio signals, arousing a sort of illusionary panic and alarm known as "the Emergency." Reviewers have praised the enigmatic plot, the puzzles and the ethical decisions and moral lessons contained within the book.

NOTES: _____

NEVER CRY WOLF, BY FARLEY MOWAT (1963) TRUE STORY, PERSONAL NARRATIVE [3]
AGE RANGE 11 - 13 YEARS / GRADE LEVEL 7 - 9 / 1330L / THEME: BIOLOGY, WOLVES

Never Cry Wolf is an account of the author's experience observing wolves in subarctic Canada. The story recounts his adventures as a biologist on a solo mission in 1946 to study Arctic wolves in the Keewatin Barren Lands in northern Manitoba and has been credited with changing the stereotypically negative perception of wolves as vicious killers. First published in 1963 it was adapted into a film of the same name in 1983.

Other books by Mowat: *The Boat Who Wouldn't Float* (1969), *People of the Deer* (1952).

NOTES: _____

NEW WORLD OF MR. TOMPKINS, THE, BY GEORGE GAMOW (AUTHOR), RUSSELL STANNARD (EDITOR), (1999) FICTION [3]
AGE RANGE 13 AND UP / GRADE LEVEL 7 AND UP / THEME: PHYSICS

This is an updated version of *Mr. Tompkins in Paperback,* the 1965 Omnibus of *Mr. Tompkins in Wonderland,* and *Mr. Tompkins Explores the Atom*. It was created by Russell Stannard in order to more correctly describe the science in the original 1930's stories that illuminate in amusing and startling fashion the oddities of, for example, Einstein's theory of relativity, bizarre effects near light-speed, the birth and death of the universe, black holes, quarks, space warps and antimatter. Mr. Tompkins in the twentieth century now embarks on some new escapades, courtesy of Stannard, who, in updating the original tales, used illustrations by Michael Edwards in Gamow's appealingly simple style. This book was not specifically written for children but would be delightful reading for a proficient reader already interested in or wondering about the physical sciences.

NOTES: _____

PAX, BY SARA PENNYPACKER (2016) FICTION [3]
AGE RANGE 9-12 / GRADE LEVEL 4-7 / 760L / THEME: ADVENTURE, RED FOX AND BOY

A compelling novel about the powerful relationship between a boy and his fox. Pax and Peter have been inseparable ever since Peter rescued him as a kit. But Peter's dad enlists in the military and makes him return the fox to the wild. This is a book that carries universal truths and is one that will touch readers of any age.

"A wilderness adventure about survival and a philosophical foray into big questions." (San Francisco Chronicle). National Book Award Longlist. New York Times Bestseller * An Amazon Best Book of the Year.

NOTES: _____

PHANTOM TOLLBOOTH, THE, BY NORTON JUSTER (1961)
FANTASY FICTION [3]
AGE RANGE 8-12 AND UP / GRADE LEVEL 3-7 / 1000L / THEME:
WORDS AND MATH

This is a children's fantasy novel. The main character Milo is transported to the Kingdom Of Wisdom, a land where harmony has been disrupted by disagreement over whether letters and numbers are equally important. The book is full of puns and literal interpretations of idioms, and has been compared to Alice's Adventures In Wonderland. Juster intended that the book speak to the importance of learning to love learning. The ideas and concepts will be enjoyed by younger readers but real understanding requires the maturity and experience of the older children. This is a book enjoyed by adults.
NOTES: _____

PRIVILEGED HANDS: A SCIENTIFIC LIFE, BY GEERAT
VERMEIJ (1996) AUTOBIOGRAPHY [3]
THIS IS AN ADULT BOOK READABLE BY AN INTERESTED 13 YEARS
OLD AND OLDER. GRADE LEVEL 8 AND UP / THEME: RESEARCH,
SHELLS, MOLLUSCS.

Blind since early childhood, the author has become a foremost evolutionary biologist using mainly his sense of touch. Dr. Vermeij is a leading authority on molluscs. His discoveries, based on feeling million-year old scarred or broken shells, have expanded our picture of how evolution works. As his fingers move across the surface of a shell, feeling the ridges and contours, searching for clues, he gathers information unnoticed by the untrained eye. For Dr. Geerat Vermeij's fingers are his eyes. He writes, "I turn each shell over in my hands, employing fingertips and nails to scrutinize all the subtleties of shape and surface ornament. ... It will prompt questions that I would not have known to ask, it will steer me to new thoughts that only firsthand observation can provoke."

Vermeij's descriptions are filled with smells, sounds, and textures. No colors, descriptions of the surrounding countryside from a sighted perspective, or descriptions of what people wore are to be found in these pages. Readers will fill in the blanks using their imaginations and forget that Vermeij uses sounds and smells to paint landscapes and events rather than sight and color. He describes how he broke into the world of ecology, malacology, and biology. He tracks his history from his days as a young blind boy growing up in post-World War II Holland through his current appointment as professor of geology at the University of California at Davis.

NOTES: _____

PROJECT MULBERRY PARK, BY LINDA SUE PARK (2005)
FICTION [3]
AGE RANGE 10-13 / GRADE LEVEL 4–6 / 690L / THEME: INSECTS, MOTHS

Seventh-grader Julia Song isn't interested in raising silkworms for her state fair project because she feels it is too Korean. However, the process of caring for the eggs, caterpillars, and moths; sewing the silk thread; and getting to know the neighbor who supplies the mulberry leaves that make her project possible changes her mind.

NOTES: _____

RISE OF THE ROCKET GIRLS, BY NATHALIA HOLT (2016) TRUE
STORIES [3]
AGE RANGE YOUNG ADULT / THEME: SCIENCE, SPACE, ENGINEERING, COMPUTERS

Rise of the Rocket Girls tells the stories of women who broke the boundaries of both gender and science in the 1940's and 50's, transformed rocket design and lay the groundwork for U.S. space travel. Based on extensive research and interviews with all the living members of the team, it tells the tales of their roles in science. What we now think of as computers hadn't been invented yet. These women spent their days writing equations and computing numbers with pencils, paper, and slide rules to give the male engineers the information they needed to build rockets, satellites, and space shuttles.

NOTES: _____

RIVER SINGERS, THE, BY TOM MOORHOUSE (2013) FICTION [3]
AGE RANGE 10 UP / GRADE LEVEL 4 UP / THEME: NATURAL HISTORY, RIVERBANKS, WATER VOLES

Tom Moorhouse, a zoology expert, has written a gripping and moving tale about four young water voles who are forced to abandon their home in the river bank and set off on a dangerous and eventful journey to find a safer place to live. Along the way they encounter many challenges and difficulties. The author weaves a fast paced adventure along with the natural history of the riverbank of the Great River located somewhere in the UK. The author lives in Oxford, UK, where he works as an ecologist at Oxford University's Zoology Department part of the Wildlife Conservation Research Unit. The voles are a seriously endangered, semiaquatic, rodent species in the UK.

NOTES: _____

ROCKET BOYS (THE COALWOOD SERIES #1), BY HOMER HICKAM (1998) MEMOIR [3]
AGE RANGE 12 AND UP / GRADE LEVEL 7 AND UP / 900L / ROCKETS, SPACE

In this memoir of a group of young men who dreamed of launching rockets into outer space, and who made those dreams come true, NASA engineer Homer Hickam tells of a time when anything seemed possible. As a high schooler Homer sees the 1957 Russian Sputnik satellite fly across the West Virginia night sky and determines to break free of the mining industry of his home town and reach for the stars with his own rockets. With the support of his teacher and three friends, he sets out to turn scrap into rockets that fly high into the sky turning his dreams into reality. This is the first of a series of three books, *Rocket Boys, The Coalwood Way,* and *Sky of Stone.*

NOTES: _____

SEA OTTER HEROES: THE PREDATORS THAT SAVED AN ECOSYSTEM, BY PATRICIA NEWMAN (2017) NONFICTION AND NARRATIVE NONFICTION [3]
AGE RANGE 9-13 / GRADE LEVEL 4-8 / 1060L / THEME: ECOLOGY, MARINE RESEARCH, SEA OTTERS

The main narrative follows marine research biologist Brent Hughes and his study of Northern California's Elkhorn Slough, which grew healthy seagrass while other inlets in similar conditions suffered. The book covers a substantiai amount of scientific detail.

NOTES: _____

SEEDFOLKS, BY PAUL FLEISCHMAN (1997) FICTION [3]
AGE RANGE 9 AND UP / GRADE LEVEL 4 UP / 710L / THEME:
BUILDING COMMUNITY AND GARDENING

A Newbery Award winning slim volume about thirteen people who gradually come together in the creation of a community garden on what had been a rat-infested vacant lot. The story takes place in the heart of the city of Cleveland in the USA. Each chapter is named for a different character and told from his or her point of view. Gardening is a sub-theme in this book that has been chosen as state and citywide read in communities across the country to celebrate the community-building aspect of the story.

NOTES: _____

SWEETNESS AT THE BOTTOM OF THE PIE, THE, BY ALAN
BRADLEY (2009) MYSTERY FICTION [3]
AGE RANGE 12 UP / GRADE LEVEL 8 UP / THEME: SCIENCE/
CHEMISTRY/EXPERIMENTATION

The author says of his 11-year-old heroine, Flavia, "She is an amalgam of burning enthusiasm, curiosity, energy, youthful idealism, and frightening fearlessness." Flavia uses scientific investigations and tactics to solve the mysteries in Bradley's stories.

Winner of the Crime Writers' Association Debut Dagger Award, the Agatha and Dilys Award and about eight other recognitions.

As of the writing of this list there are eight more books in the series: *#2-The Weed That Strings the Hangman's Bag, #3-A Red Herring Without Mustard, #4-I Am Half-Sick of Shadows, #5-Speaking From Among The Bones, #6-The Dead in Their Vaulted Arches, #7-As Chimney Sweepers Come to Dust, #8-Thrice the Brinded Cat Hath Mew'd, #9-The Grave's a Fine and Private Place.*

NOTES: _____

TALES FROM WATERSHIP DOWN, BY RICHARD ADAMS (1996)
FICTION [3]
AGE RANGE 9-12 / GRADE LEVEL 4-7 / THEME: FICTION, NATURE
VERSUS MANKIND, ANIMALS, RABBITS.

This is a sequel to *Watership Down* and introduces some new rabbit characters to join in the struggles and adventures of Fiver, Hazel, Bigwig, Dandelion, and the legendary hero Elahrairah. Adams was a

British novelist best known for *Watership Down, Shardik,* and *The Plague Dogs*.

NOTES: _____

THERE'S A HAIR IN MY DIRT! A WORM'S STORY, BY GARY LARSON (1998) FICTION [3]
AGE RANGE 10-13 / GRADE LEVEL 6-8 / 640L / THEME: BIOLOGY, CYCLE OF LIFE

Written and illustrated in a children's storybook style, *There's a Hair in My Dirt! A Worm's Story* is a twisted take on the difference between our idealized view of Nature and the sometimes cold, hard reality of life for the birds and the bees and the worms (not to mention our own species). While the author spent a career lifetime as a comic cartoonist he was an avowed environmentalist. The foreword is by Edward O. Wilson.

NOTES: _____

TIME AND SPACE OF UNCLE ALBERT, THE, BY RUSSELL STANNARD (1989) FICTION [3]
AGE RANGE 9-12 / GRADE LEVEL 4-6 / THEME: PHYSICS, LIGHT

Uncle Albert and his niece Gedanken unravel and reveal abstract concepts through a computer and a spacecraft that allow her to travel in time and space.

Uncle Albert is a famous scientist, and it's his imagination that sends Gedanken into the dangerous and unknown world of a thought bubble to examine near light-speed phenomena.

The Time and Space of Uncle Albert is book one in the Uncle Albert science and adventure series. Book two is *Uncle Albert and the Quantum Test*.

NOTES: _____

TOWN SECRETS, (THE BOOK OF ADAM 1), BY SCOTT GELOWITZ (2014) SCIENCE FICTION [3]
AGE RANGE 10-13 / GRADE LEVEL 4-6 / THEME: FANTASY SF

A science fiction adventure series set in the author's small prairie hometown of Grayson, Saskatchewan, Canada. The town is real, the characters are not.

Four boys uncover mythical and scientific secrets that tie their boring small town to historical events from around the world. One of those secrets could be the reason nearby towns are being destroyed —and thirteen-year-old Adam may be the only one able to protect the biggest secret of all.

NOTES: _____

UNDER THE EGG, BY LAURA MARX FITZGERALD (2014)
FICTION [3]
AGE RANGE 9–12 / GRADE LEVEL 4–7. / 790L / THEME: ART MYSTERY, PROBLEM SOLVING, ADVENTURE

Thirteen-year-old Theo accidentally discovers another painting hiding under one by her artist grandfather. When she spills a bottle of rubbing alcohol on the painting, she discovers what seems to be an old Renaissance masterpiece underneath. The more she learns about it, the more she suspects it might be an actual Renaissance masterpiece. But if it's genuine, that would only raise a new series of questions, such as how her grandfather came to have it and whether it's stolen. With surprising twists, heartwarming moments, historical facts, and revealing information about both art and science, this is an intriguing mystery adventure. Sequel: *The Gallery*.

NOTES: _____

UNTAMED: THE WILD LIFE OF JANE GOODALL, BY ANITA SILVEY, FOREWORD BY JANE GOODALL (2015) BIOGRAPHY [3]
AGE RANGE 10-14 YEARS / GRADE LEVEL 4–9 / 110L / THEME: BIOGRAPHY, PRIMATE SCIENTIST

A National Geographic Kids Book featuring gorgeous, full-color photographs, primary sources, and fun nature facts. Goodall is presented as inspiring and intelligent as well as down-to-earth in her personality and methods. This is the fascinating story of the child-hood and career of a famed scientist and has a foreword by the scientist, Jane Goodall, and a great many photographs of her early years and fieldwork-studying chimpanzees in Africa.

NOTES: _____

WATER SKY, BY JEAN CRAIGHEAD GEORGE (1987) FICTION [3]
AGE RANGE 10 AND UP / GRADE LEVEL: 6-8 / 730L / THEME:
CONSERVATION, ALASKA, WHALES

Nothing in teenager Lincoln Stonewright's past experience quite prepares him for the whaling camp at Barrow. Here ice is a living presence and the temperature is so cold that spilled water hits the ground as ice balls. The engaging, suspenseful story is a blend of Eskimo ritual and modern science.

NOTES: _____

WAY WE FALL, THE, BY MEGAN CREW (2012) FICTION [3]
AGE RANGE 12 AND UP / GRADE LEVEL 7-12 / 770L / THEME:
MICROBIOLOGY SCIENCE THRILLER

This is a science thriller, not 'science fiction'. The story takes place in our world and time. It's not hard to imagine the events that take place in this fictional account actually occurring. The story is told by 16-year-old Kaelyn in the form of letters to a friend. Kaelyn lives in a small island community on Lake Ontario near Toronto. The community is struck by a lethal virus and is quarantined as people die and society begins to unravel. *The Way We Fall* is book one in a 4-book Fallen World series.

NOTES: _____

THE WESTING GAME, BY ELLEN RASKIN (1978) FICTION [3]
AGE RANGE 8–12 YEARS / GRADE LEVEL 3–7 / 750L / THEME:
PROBLEM SOLVING, ADVENTURE

This highly inventive mystery involves a group of people who are invited to live in the Sunset Towers apartment building and to the reading of Samuel W. Westing's will. The will challenges them to solve Westing's murder. They split up into eight pairs, each pair being given a set of clues and $10,000 dollars to play the game. They could become millionaires-it all depends on how they play the tricky and dangerous game involving blizzards, burglaries, and bombings! Ellen Raskin has created a remarkable cast of characters in a problem solving, puzzle-knotted, word-twisting plot filled with humor, intrigue, and suspense.

Winner of the Newbery Medal, the Boston Globe/Horn Book Award, and an ALA Notable Book.

NOTES: _____

WHAT COLOR IS MY WORLD?: THE LOST HISTORY OF AFRICAN-AMERICAN INVENTORS, BY KAREEM ABDUL-JABBAR (2012) NONFICTION WITHIN FICTION [3]
AGE RANGE 8 AND UP / GRADE LEVEL 3 AND UP/ 880L / THEME: INVENTION

Kareem Abdul-Jabbar, basketball legend and the NBA's all-time leading scorer, champions a lineup of little-known African-American inventors in this lively, kid-friendly book. With Fast-fact profiles and framed by a funny contemporary story featuring two feisty twins, this is an introduction to the minds behind the gamma electric cell and the ice-cream scoop, improvements to traffic lights, open-heart surgery, and more—inventors whose ingenuity and perseverance against great odds made our world safer, better, and brighter.
NOTES: _____

WRINKLE IN TIME, A, BY MADELINE L'ENGLE (1962) FICTION [3]
AGE RANGE 10-14 YEARS / GRADE LEVEL 4-6 / 740L / THEME: FANTASY SCIENCE FICTION

Madeleine L'Engle introduced the world to the two children, Meg and Charles Wallace Murry, and their friend Calvin O'Keefe. When the children learn that Mr. Murry has been captured by the Dark Thing, they time travel to Camazotz, where they must face the leader IT in the ultimate battle between good and evil–a journey that threatens their lives and our universe. *A Wrinkle in Time* is the winner of the 1963 Newbery Medal. It is the first book in The Time Quintet, which consists of *A Wrinkle in Time, A Wind in the Door, A Swiftly Tilting Planet, Many Waters,* and *An Acceptable Time*. The stories follow the Murry family's continuing experiences and adventures involving time travel, fantasy and struggles between good and evil. L'Engle created her different universes after reading about Einstein's theories concerning our own universe.
NOTES: _____

"A book is a garden, an orchard, a storehouse, a party, a company by the way, a counselor, a multitude of counselors."

–CHARLES BAUDELAIRE

ADVANCED READER STORIES

3:59, BY GRETCHEN MCNEIL (2013) SCIENCE FICTION [4]
AGE RANGE: YOUNG ADULT / THEME: SCIENCE FICTION, ALTERNATE UNIVERSES.

A scientifically action-packed story about an alternate universe. A portal to an alternate reality opens at precisely 3:59 through teenager Josie's bedroom mirror. There is suspense and a splash of horror in this story that makes it less suitable for younger readers but quite suitable for young adults.

NOTES: _____

40 SIGNS OF RAIN, BY KIM STANLEY ROBINSON (2004)
FICTION [4]
ADULT AND YOUNG ADULT / THEME: ENVIRONMENTAL DISASTER

Hauntingly realistic, here is a novel, by the bestselling author of the classic Mars trilogy, of the near future that is inspired by scientific facts already making headlines. Senate environmental staffer Charlie Quibler deals with the frustrating politics of global warming. Charlie must find a way to get a skeptical administration to act before it's too late. His portrayal of how actual scientists would deal with this disaster-in-the making is convincing.

NOTES: _____

AIRBORN, BY KENNETH OPPEL (2004) STEAMPUNK FICTION [4]
AGE RANGE 12 AND UP / GRADE LEVEL 6-10 / THEME: AIRSHIPS, ZOOLOGY.

Airborn is a 2004 young adult novel set in an alternate history where the airplane has not been invented, and instead, airships are the primary form of air transportation. The world of the story contains fictional animal species such as flying creatures, which live their entire lives in the sky. The tale is told from the perspective of the airship Aurora's cabin boy, Matt Cruse. This is Book 1 in Oppel's Matt Cruse Series.

NOTES: _____

AN ABUNDANCE OF KATHERINES BY JOHN GREEN (2006)
MATHEMATICS FICTION [4]
YOUNG ADULT / 890L / THEME MATHEMATICS

An Abundance Of Katherines is a young adult novel with a math-loving protagonist named Colin. Colin uses mathematical equations throughout the novel, some of which are explained in the book's appendix by mathematician Daniel Biss. A 2007 Michael L. Prinz Honor book, finalist for the Los Angeles Times Book Prize, named one of the books of the year by Booklist, Horn Book, and Kirkus.

NOTES: _____

ARCHANGEL, BY ANDREA BARRETT (2013) FICTION, SHORT STORIES [4]
AN ADULT BOOK READABLE BY INTERESTED YOUNG ADULTS OF 15 AND UP / THEME: SCIENCE AND NATURE

Winner of the National Book Award for her collection of stories *Ship Fever*, Andrea Barrett's *Archangel* unfolds five significant moments in the lives of her characters and each is set at a moment of decisive scientific change. The five fictional events occur in 1908, 1920, 1873, and 1919. They are rich with scientific fact and Barrett explores the thrill and sense of loss that come with scientific progress and the personal passions and impersonal politics that shape all human knowledge. The themes include cave-dwelling fish, scientifically bred crops, motorized bicycles, the flight of an early aeroplane, evolution, genetics, and X-ray technology.

NOTES: _____

ASHFALL, BY MIKE MULLIN (2010) FICTION [4]
AGE RANGE 14 AND UP / GRADE LEVEL 8 AND UP / THEME: GEOLOGY, YELLOWSTONE PARK CALIFORNIA.

Under the bubbling hot springs and geysers of Yellowstone National Park is a super-volcano. It just could be overdue for an eruption, which would change the landscape and climate of our planet. Alex is alone for the weekend. Then the Yellowstone supervolcano erupts, plunging his hometown into a nightmare of darkness, ash, and violence. Alex begins a harrowing trek to search for his family. This is Book 1 of 1 in the Ashfall Trilogy Series. [Alert: This is a riveting tale of survival and is more appropriate for older teens due to some violence.]

NOTES: _____

BILLION DOLLAR MOLECULE, THE, ONE COMPANY'S QUEST FOR THE PERFECT DRUG, BY BARRY WERTH (1995)
NON FICTION [4+]
AN ADULT BOOK READABLE BY INTERESTED YOUNG ADULTS OF 15 AND UP.

From test tubes to Wall Street and beyond, this is the true story of a start-up pharmaceutical company working to create an anti-AIDS drug. Scientifically accurate, yet written with an attention to plot, timing, dialogue, and development of character more characteristic of the best thrillers. In 2014 Werth published *Antidote,* a sequel to this story.

NOTES: _____

BOAT WHO WOULDN'T FLOAT, THE, BY FARLEY MOWAT
(1969) TRUE STORY, PERSONAL NARRATIVE [4]
AGE RANGE 12 AND UP / GRADE LEVEL 7 AND UP / THEME: NAUTICAL,

'The Happy Adventure' was a schooner with one fatal flaw. It leaked like a sieve. So why would anyone repeatedly expose himself and his friends to the elements of the North Atlantic in a treacherous, stubborn, uncomfortable, unfloatable boat? But the story is true. And it's one of the funniest stories ever from Farley Mowat. Farley McGill Mowat (1921-2014) was author of more than forty books; he was a popular and distinguished naturalist and conservationist whose internationally acclaimed novels, and books for young readers have been translated into fifty-two languages. Mowat's other books include: *People of the Deer; Lost in the Barrens,* which was a recipient of Canada's Governor General's Award.

NOTES: _____

CERTAIN AMBIGUITY, A, A MATHEMATICAL NOVEL, BY GAURAV SURI AND HARTOSH BAL (2007) MATHEMATICAL FICTION [4]
YOUNG ADULT AND ADULT / THEME: MATHEMATICS

Winner of the 2007 Award for Best Professional/Scholarly Book in Mathematics, the book is a delightful and informative read. It is a human story about mathematics, about its philosophy, its beauty and about its relevance to the human understanding of the surrounding world. This is a novel but mathematics is woven inextricably into the story line.

NOTES: _____

DOUBLE HELIX, THE, BY JAMES D. WATSON (1968)
NONFICTION [4]
AGE RANGE 15 TO ADULT / GRADE LEVEL 9 AND UP / THEME: BIOPHYSICS, DNA, SCIENCE DISCOVERY

The Double Helix describes, in breezy and very readable prose, the discovery, by James Watson and Francis Crick, of the helical structure of the DNA (Deoxyribonucleic acid) molecule present in all living cells. The book has been described as containing not a solemn or pompous word but instead being full of gossipy vignettes. However, the book is often criticized by the scientific community for focusing too much on the glory of 'being first' and for short-changing the essential, complementary work of others. A recent publication, *The Annotated and Illustrated Double Helix* by James D. Watson, edited by Alex Gann and Jan Witkowski, was published to mark the fiftieth anniversary of the 1962 Nobel Prize for Watson and Crick's discovery. This special edition of Watson's autobiography does not change the original text but gives new insights into personal relationships and Rosalind Franklin and has been favorably reviewed.

(Listed in this bibliography is *My Sister Rosalind Franklin* by Jennifer Glynn.)

NOTES: _____

ELEPHANT WHISPERER, THE, BY LAWRENCE ANTHONY (2009)
TRUE STORY, PERSONAL NARRATIVE [4]
AGE RANGE YOUNG ADULT AND ADULT / THEME: CONSERVATION, AFRICAN WILDLIFE, ELEPHANTS.

A heartwarming, exciting, funny, and sometimes sad account of

Anthony's experiences with a herd of rogue elephants. Set against the background of life on an African game reserve. Lawrence Anthony the owner of Thula Thula a conservationist game sanctuary in Zululand, South Africa was a passionate conservationist. When Anthony died the elephants assembled outside his home in accordance with the way elephants usually mourn the death of one of their own.

Anthony wrote two other true-life stories. *Babylon's Ark*, the wartime rescue of the Baghdad zoo, is an emotional, perhaps difficult, true story for children. *The Last Rhino*, is a powerful story of one man's battle to save a species.

NOTES: _____

FLATLAND: A ROMANCE OF MANY DIMENSIONS, BY
EDWIN ABBOTT (1884) FICTION [4]
YOUNG ADULT AND ADULT / THEME: MATHEMATICS, SATIRE

First published in 1884 this satirical novel by an English schoolmaster is an adventure in mathematics. The story's protagonist is "A Square" who lives in a fictional two-dimensional world that is intended to represent Victorian society and culture but the more enduring contribution is its examination of mathematical dimensions. While the story can be read be read simply as a humorous, whimsical tale the underlying intent is a criticism of people and society. Young adult readers who enjoy mathematical ideas should find this an enjoyable read. Adults are more likely to understand the satire.

A feature film, "Flatland" (2007), has been made from the story. Several short or experimental films include one narrated by Dudley Moore.

NOTES: _____

GALILEO'S DAUGHTER, BY DAVA STOBEL (2000)
NONFICTION [4]
AGE RANGE: AN ADULT BOOK SUITABLE FOR INTERESTED, GOOD READERS OF 15 AND UP / THEME: ASTRONOMY

In *Galileo's Daughter*, Dava Sobel tells the story of the famous Italian physicist and astronomer and Sister Maria Celeste the oldest of his three illegitimate children. Sobel's story is more about Galileo than his daughter but, by including the 124 surviving letters to the scientist from his daughter, Sobel augments the story with life of that time period and place revealing the agonies of the bubonic plague, the hardships of monastic life, even Galileo's occasional forgetfulness ("The little basket, which I sent you recently with several pastries, is not mine, and therefore I wish you to return it to me").

Dava Sobel's previous book was *Longitude*, about John Harrison, an 18th-century clockmaker who created the first clock (chronometer) sufficiently accurate to be used to determine longitude at sea -without longitude, ships often found themselves so far off course that sailors would starve or die of scurvy before they could reach port.

NOTES: _____

HIDDEN FIGURES, BY MARGOT LEE SHETTERLY (2016) FACT-BASED FICTION [4]
ADULT AND YOUNG ADULT / THEME: SPACE, MATHEMATICS

In *Hidden Figures: The American Dream and the Untold Story of the Black Women Mathematicians Who Helped Win the Space Race,* Margot Lee Shetterly follows the interwoven accounts of Dorothy Vaughan, Mary Jackson, Katherine Johnson and Christine Darden, four African American women who participated in some of NASA's greatest successes. These women were part a group made up of mostly women who calculated by hand the complex equations that allowed space heroes like Neil Armstrong, Alan Shepard, and John Glenn to travel safely to space. This is a book written for adult readers and suitable for interested young adults. Shetterly has published two other Hidden Figures books: *Hidden Figures Young Readers' Edition* (2016), and *Hidden Figures: The True Story of Four Black Women and the Space Race*, Picture Book edition (2018). Both of these are very readable but presented more as nonfiction than narrative story.

NOTES: _____

KING SOLOMON'S RING, BY KONRAD LORENZ (1949)
NONFICTION [4]
AGE RANGE TEEN AND ADULT / THEME: ANIMAL BEHAVIOR

The title reference to Solomon refers to the legend that King Solomon (about 950 CBE) had a magic ring that enabled him to speak to the animals in their own language. Lorenz was gifted with a similar power of understanding the animal world. He was a brilliant scientist and received a Nobel Prize for his work. *King Solomon's*

Ring is a delightful treasury of observations and insights into the lives of all sorts of creatures, from jackdaws and water-shrews to dogs, cats and even wolves.

NOTES: _____

LAB GIRL, BY HOPE JAHREN (2016) AUTOBIOGRAPHICAL
TRUE STORY [4]
AN ADULT BOOK SUITABLE FOR YOUNG ADULTS AGE 14 AND UP / THEME: BIOLOGY, BOTANY

In her memoir *Lab Girl*, Hope Jahren describes the life she's lived and the knowledge she's learned as a scientist trying to find her way in the world. Jahren is a geobiologist and has spent her life studying trees, flowers, seeds, and soil. *Lab Girl* is about plant life—but it is also a celebration of the lifelong curiosity, humility, and passion that drive every scientist. Jahren is the recipient of three Fulbright Awards and is the only woman, to have been awarded both of the Young Investigator Medals given within the Earth Sciences.

NOTES: _____

LIFE AS WE KNEW IT, BY SUSAN BETH PFEFFER (2006) YOUNG
ADULT, SCIENCE FICTION NOVEL [4]
AGE RANGE 12 AND UP / GRADE LEVEL 7-9 / THEME: APOCALYPSE SURVIVAL

When an asteroid hits the moon and brings it closer to Earth, life in Northeastern Pennsylvania will never be the same again for Miranda and her family, with the lack of food and extreme cold major threats to their survival. Life As We Knew It is the first book in Pfeffer's The Last Survivors series: *Life as We Knew It* (2006), *The Dead and the Gone* (2008), *This World We Live In* (2010), *The Shade of the Moon* (2013)

NOTES: _____

LAST DAYS OF NIGHT, THE, BY GRAHAM MOORE (2017)
NARRATIVE NONFICTION [4]
AN ADULT BOOK READABLE BY INTERESTED YOUNG ADULTS OF 15 AND UP / THEME: PHYSICS, ELECTRICITY

Graham Moor has created a very engaging novel—based on actual events—about the nature of genius, the state of electrical technology at the time of the story, and the personal and legal battle to electrify America. The date is 1888. The location is New York. The main players are Thomas Edison, George Westinghouse, Nikola Tesla, and J.P. Morgan. The protagonist is a young, untested attorney named Paul Cravath. The legal question is, "Who invented the light bulb and holds the right to power the country?" Moore has drawn believable characters and scenarios and in several pages at the end of the book explains that the story is a dramatization of history, not a recording of it and that the main events depicted did happen and the major characters and their dialogues were real.

NOTES: _____

MAN MEETS DOG, BY KONRAD LORENZ (1949) NONFICTION [4]
AGE RANGE TEEN / ADULT / THEME: ANIMAL BEHAVIOR

In this fine book, the famous scientist, Konrad Lorenz, 'the man who talked with animals', enlightens and entertains us with his account of the relationships between humans and their pets. With Lorenz's customary humanity and expert knowledge, Man Meets Dog is a personal and entertaining account of his relationships with his own four-legged friends. With charming sketches on almost every page, *Man Meets Dog* offers a delightful insight into animal and human thinking and feeling.

NOTES: _____

MARTIAN, THE, BY ANDY WEIR (2012) SCIENCE FICTION [4]
AGE RANGE ADULTS AND TEENS / THEME: SPACE, MARS

In 2035 Mark Watney was one of the first people to walk on Mars as part of the crew of the NASA Ares 3 mission. After a wild storm the crew were ordered to evacuate but left Mark behind thinking him to be dead. But he is not. Mark finds himself stranded and completely alone with no way to even signal Earth that he's alive—and even if he could get word out, his supplies would be gone long before a rescue could arrive. A good, original story, interestingly real characters and fascinating technical accuracy.

NOTES: _____

MICROBE HUNTERS, THE, BY PAUL DE KRUIF (1926)
NONFICTION [4]
AGE RANGE TEEN / ADULT / THEME: MICROBIOLOGY

This science classic by Paul de Kruif is a timeless dramatization of the pioneering bacteriological work of such scientists as Leeuwenhoek, Spallanzani, Koch, Pasteur, Reed, and Ehrlich. These men discovered microbes and invented the vaccines to counter them. De Kruif describes simple but fundamental discoveries of science—how a microbe was first viewed in a clear drop of rain water, and when, for the first time ever, Louis Pasteur discovered that a simple vaccine could save a man from the ravages of rabies by attacking the microbes that cause it.

NOTES: _____

PASSION FOR SCIENCE, A, BY LEWIS WOLPERT AND ALISON RICHARDS (1988) NONFICTION [4]
AGE RANGE YOUNG ADULT / THEME: DISCOVERING SCIENCE

A Passion for Science features thirteen conversations with eminent scientists who speak with candor and good humor about what they find most rewarding about their work, and what it feels like to make a major discovery. Stephen Jay Gould comments that he is not a particularly good deductive thinker nor mathematically inclined, but excellent at finding hidden connections. Nobel Laureate Abdus Salam reveals that he became a scientist by chance. Tony Epstein, co-discoverer of the Epstein-Barr Virus says of his reaction to seeing the virus for the first time, "I switched the microscope off...and I went out and walked round the block two or three times before I dared come back!"

NOTES: _____

PETROPLAGUE, BY AMY ROGERS (2011) FICTION [4]
YOUNG ADULT AND ADULT / THEME: SCIENCE THRILLER, MICROBIOLOGY

Petroplague is a novel with real science about oil-eating bacteria that contaminate the fuel supply. It's packed with accurate chemistry, microbiology, ecology, geology, and important social themes answering the implied question, What would happen if a petroleum-destroying plague got loose? In Rogers' science thriller nothing that runs on gasoline moves. Instability under the Santa Monica fault leads to bigger and bigger earthquakes. The La Brea Tar Pits erupt. This very readable thriller based on valid science is appropriate for grades 9-12 and up. Rogers second book published in 2014 was *Reversion,* a science thriller about gene therapy.

NOTES: _____

PRACTICE EFFECT, THE, BY DAVID BRIN (1984)
SCIENCE FICTION [4]
AGE RANGE: 14 AND UP GRADE LEVEL: 9-12 /THEME: PHYSICS, TIME AND SPACE

In this 1984 novel, scientists succeed in creating a device, called the "Zievatron", that manipulates space and time — and they're able to use it to travel to another planet, which is very similar to Earth. Except on this other planet, the second law of thermodynamics works differently: Objects don't get worn out, and in fact get stronger the longer they're used. This is referred to as the Practice effect. It's up to Dennis Nuel to figure out why this aberration is happening. David Brin is a scientist. He has a doctorate in astrophysics and has been a NASA consultant and a physics professor.

NOTES: _____

RATS, BY ROBERT SULLIVAN (2004)
PERSONAL EXPERIENCE NONFICTION STORY [4]
AGE RANGE 14 AND UP / GRADE LEVEL 8 AND UP / THEME: NATURAL HISTORY OF A CITY, RATS

Robert Sullivan spent a year investigating a rat-infested alley just a few blocks away from Wall Street. Sullivan got to know not just the beast but its friends and foes: the exterminators, the sanitation workers, the agitators and activists who have played their part in the centuries-old war between human city dweller and wild city rat. A funny, wise, best seller, sometimes disgusting but always readable. This book was a New York Public Library Book for the Teen Age • A New York Public Library Book to Remember; A PSLA Young Adult Top 40 nonfiction title 2004.

NOTES: _____

SEEDS: A POST-APOCALYPTIC ADVENTURE, BY CHRIS MANDEVILLE (2015) SCIENCE FICTION [4]
AGE RANGE: 14 AND ADULT / GRADE LEVEL: 8 AND UP / THEME: POST APOCALYPTIC SURVIVAL.

Forty-eight years after a catastrophic solar event destroys all life and technology on the planet's surface, nineteen-year-old Reid Landers, his colony's medic, lives in the old NORAD facility deep inside Cheyenne Mountain with other descendants of Originals. They barely subsist on canned food and rats. For all they know, they are the last hundred

souls on Earth...until Reid meets a stranger with a grown apple. This sends him on a journey to California to find seeds for his people.
NOTES: _____

SERVANTS OF THE MAP, BY ANDREA BARRETT (2002)
FICTION, SHORT STORIES [4]
AN ADULT BOOK READABLE BY INTERESTED YOUNG ADULTS OF 15 AND UP / THEME: SCIENCE AND NATURE

The stories range across two centuries, and from the western Himalaya to an Adirondack village. A mapper of the highest mountain peaks realizes his true obsession. A young woman afire with scientific curiosity must come to terms with a romantic fantasy. Brothers and sisters, torn apart at an early age, are beset by dreams of reunion. Readers of *Ship Fever* (National Book Award winner) and *The Voyage of the Narwhal* will discover subtle links both among these stories and to characters in the earlier works. (Selected for Best American Short Stories (2001) and The O. Henry Awards (2001).)
NOTES: _____

SHELL COLLECTOR, THE, BY ANTHONY DOERR (2001) FICTION, SHORT STORIES [4]
AN ADULT BOOK READABLE BY INTERESTED YOUNG ADULTS OF 15 AND UP / THEME: SCIENCE AND NATURE

From the African Coast to the pine forests of Montana to the damp moors of Lapland, charting a vast physical and emotional landscape, Doerr explores the human condition in all its varieties conjuring nature in both its beautiful abundance and crushing power. Some of the characters in these stories contend with hardships; some discover unique gifts; all are united by their ultimate deference to the ravishing universe outside themselves.
NOTES: _____

SHIP BREAKER, BY PAOLO BACIGALUPI (2010) FICTION [4]
AGE RANGE 13 AND UP / GRADE LEVEL 7 AND UP/ THEME GLOBAL WARMING, OIL.

Ship Breaker is a young adult novel set in a dark, post-apocalyptic future. Human civilization is in decline for ecological reasons. The polar ice caps have melted and New Orleans is underwater. In America's Gulf Coast region, where grounded oil tankers are being broken down for parts, Nailer, a teenage boy, works the light crew, scavenging for copper wiring just to make quota--and hopefully live to see another day.

This is Book 1 in the Ship Breaker Series and was a finalist for the 2010 National Book Award for Young People's Literature.

NOTES: _____

SHIP FEVER, BY ANDREA BARRETT (1996) FICTION, SHORT STORIES [4]
AN ADULT BOOK READABLE BY INTERESTED YOUNG ADULTS OF 15 AND UP / THEME: SCIENCE AND NATURE

In this 1996 National Book Award Winner for Fiction the eloquent short fictions concerning varieties of scientific pursuit and discovery tell about the love of science and the science of love. Interweaving historical and fictional characters, they encompass both past and present. In *Ship Fever,* the title novella, a young Canadian doctor finds himself at the center of one of history's most tragic epidemics. In *The English Pupil* Linnaeus, in old age, watches as the world he organized within his head slowly drifts beyond his reach. And in *The Littoral Zone* two marine biologists wonder whether their life-altering affair finally was worth it. "Science is transformed from hard and known fact into malleable, strange and thrilling fictional material" (Boston Globe).

NOTES: _____

STORY OF CHARLOTTE'S WEB, THE, BY MICHAEL SIMS (2011) NONFICTION [4]
AGE RANGE TEEN AND ADULT / THEME: BIOGRAPHY

While composing what would become his most enduring and popular book, E. B. White obeyed the maxim: "Write what you know." Helpless pigs, silly geese, clever spiders, greedy rats. White knew all of these characters in the barns and stables where he spent his favorite hours as a child and adult. Michael Sims chronicles White's animal-rich childhood, his writing about urban nature for the New Yorker, his scientific research into how spiders spin webs and lay eggs, the composition and publication of his masterpiece, and his ongoing quest to recapture an enchanted childhood.

NOTES: _____

UNCLE TUNGSTEN, BY OLIVER SACKS (2001) MEMOIR [4]
AN ADULT BOOK VERY SUITABLE FOR HIGH SCHOOL AGES 15-18 /
THEME: CHEMISTRY

Uncle Tungsten: Memories of a Chemical Boyhood radiates Sacks'
boyhood delight and wonder as he discovered science through
personal experience with his family's wide ranging science connections. The story is an amalgamation of science, chemistry, history,
family, and personal reflection in which Sacks tells how his large,
science-steeped family fostered his early fascination with chemistry.
He tells of his joy of scientific understanding; what it is like to be a
precocious child discovering the alchemical secrets of reality for the
first time; the sheer thrill of finding intelligible patterns in nature and
of his young years at boarding school where he further developed
the intellectual curiosity that would shape his later life.
NOTES: _____

VOYAGE OF THE NARWHAL, THE, BY ANDREA BARRETT
(1998) FICTION [4]
AN ADULT BOOK READABLE BY INTERESTED YOUNG ADULTS OF 15
AND UP / THEME: SCIENCE AND NATURE

In this novel Andrea Barratt captures a crucial moment in the history
of exploration—the mid-nineteenth century romance with the
Arctic—and tells the story of a fateful expedition through the eyes of
the ship's scholar-naturalist, Erasmus Darwin Wells. *The Voyage of
the Narwhal* is a gripping adventure story. A motley crew of men
sets off for the Arctic in 1855 looking for traces of Sir John Franklin's
expedition of a decade before. We encounter the Narwhal's crew, its
commander, and the far-north culture of the Esquimaux. In counter-
point, are the women left behind in Philadelphia, explorers only in
imagination.
NOTES: _____

WATERSHIP DOWN, BY RICHARD ADAMS (1972) FICTION [4]
AGE RANGE 12 AND UP THROUGH ADULT / GRADE LEVEL 7 AND UP /
THEME: FICTION, NATURE VERSUS MANKIND, ANIMALS, RABBITS

This enduring classic is set in England's Downs. It is an imaginative
tale, written for adults but appropriate for older children, of the
courage, adventure, and survival of an anthropomorphic colony of
wild rabbits as they flee from the intrusion of humans and the

certain destruction of their home. The characters are based on people that Adams knew but Adams says he never made the rabbits do anything physical that rabbits cannot do. The rabbit behaviors were vetted by R.M. Lockley a well-known naturalist. Adams made up the story for his children on car drives and bedtime storytelling; they encouraged him to write it down and have it made into a book for others to share. It's a thick book but engrossing. *Watership Down* was a winner of the Carnegie Medal and the Guardian Award for Children's Literature. See also the sequel, *Tales from Watership Down*.

NOTES: _____

WIZARD OF QUARKS, THE, BY ROBERT GILMORE (2001)
FANTASY FICTION [4]
AGE RANGE YOUNG ADULT 15 YRS. PLUS AND ADULT / THEME FANTASY OF PARTICLE PHYSICS

Physicist Robert Gilmore takes readers on a journey with Dorothy, following the yellow brick road through the land of the Wizard of Quarks. Gilmore uses characters and situations based on the Wizard of Oz story. Classes of particles, from quarks to leptons are shown in an atomic garden, where atoms and molecules are produced. Dorothy, The Tin Geek, and the Cowardly Lion experience the bizarre world of subatomic particles.

Robert Gilmore is a lecturer in physics at Bristol University in England and has worked in particle physics at Brookhaven, Stanford, and CERN. Also by Gilmore; *Alice in Quantumland—An allegory of Quantum Physics;* and, *Scrooge's Cryptic Carol—Visions of Energy, Time and Quantum Nature.*

NOTES: _____

Science Graphic Novels

Graphic Novels with Science in the Story

Ages 12 up, grades 7 up; includes fiction and nonfiction stories in comic format.

____*Adventures of Mr. Thompkins, The, Volume 1,* by Igor Gamow — Graphic novel [3]

____*Charles Darwin's On the Origin of Species,* by Michael Keller — Graphic novel [4]

____*Clan Apis,* by Jay Hosler — Nonfiction graphic novel [3]

____*Dialogues, The,* by Clifford Johnson — Graphic novel [4]

____*Last of the Sandwalkers,* by Jay Hosler — Nonfiction graphic novel [2]

____*Neurocomic,* by Hana Ros, illustrated by Matteo Farinella — Graphic novel [4]

____*Primates, Fearless Science of Jane Goodall, Dian Fossey, and Birute Galdikas,* by Jim Ottaviani — True story, Nonfiction graphic novel [3]

____*Science: A Discovery in Comics,* by Margreet de Heer — Nonfiction graphic novel [4]

____*Secret Science Alliance and the Copycat Crook, The,* by Eleanor Davis — Graphic novel [2]

____*T-Minus: The Race to the Moon,* by Jim Ottaviani — True story, Graphic novel [3]

Descriptions for the Science Graphic Novels

ADVENTURES OF MR. THOMPKINS, THE, BY IGOR GAMOW
(2010) GRAPHIC NOVEL [3]
AGE RANGE 13 AND UP / GRADE LEVEL 7 AND UP / THEME: PHYSICS

This is the first of Igor Gamow's graphic-novel series written based on his father's popular books of the 1930's. Mr. Tompkins, the title character, an inquisitive bank clerk created by physicist George Gamow in 1937, returns in a new comic format by Igor Gamow. The books are structured as a series of dreams in which Tompkins enters alternative worlds where the physical constants have radically different values from those they have in the real world. In his dreams Mr. Thompkins learns about gravity from Albert Einstein, explores the atom with Ernest Rutherford and gets a radioactive guided tour by Marie Curie. This first volume is based on George Gamow's 1939 book *Mr. Thompkins in Wonderland*. (A second volume, based on *Mr. Thompkins explores the Atom*, in which Tompkins meets Charles Darwin, Gregor Mendel, and James Watson, was published in July 2011.)

The author, Igor Gamow, says: "When I first joined the faculty at the University of Colorado in 1967 as a professor of engineering, our high school students rated number one in amongst the 30 industrial countries–today our students are 35th! Our proposed science series has been designed to inspire students, through education and entertainment to restore our previous status."

NOTES: _____

CHARLES DARWIN'S ON THE ORIGIN OF SPECIES; A GRAPHIC ADAPTATION, BY MICHAEL KELLER (2009)
NONFICTION GRAPHIC NOVEL [4]
AGE RANGE 14 AND UP / GRADE LEVEL 9 UP / THEME: ORIGIN OF SPECIES

"A stunning graphic adaptation of one of the most famous, contested, and important books of all time." –Amazon.

This novel introduces readers to some of Darwin's original text. Including sections about his pioneering research and his correspondence with other leading scientists, as well as the most recent breakthroughs in evolutionary theory. For purposes of helping to define the age appropriateness it should be noted that while large portions of the book are characterized by conversation as in a storytelling mode a good percentage of the book is presented in a more informational manner.

NOTES: _____

CLAN APIS, BY JAY HOSLER (2000) NONFICTION GRAPHIC NOVEL [3]
AGE RANGE 10-13 / GRADE LEVEL 5-7 / THEME: BEE BIOLOGY

Clan Apis is the biography of a honey bee named Nyuki told in comic book form. Written and drawn by biologist Jay Hosler, Clan Apis is an elegant blend of humor, storytelling, and scientifically accurate information regarding honey bee biology and natural history.

NOTES: _____

DIALOGUES, THE, BY CLIFFORD JOHNSON (2017) GRAPHIC NOVEL [4]
AN ADULT COMIC BOOK SUITABLE FOR YOUNG ADULTS AGE 14 AND UP / THEME: SCIENCE CONVERSATIONS BASED ON REAL SCIENCE

Physicist Clifford Johnson thinks that we should have more conversations about science. In The Dialogues, Johnson lets us to eavesdrop on nine conversations, that take place all over the world, in museums, on trains, in restaurants. The conversationalists are men, women, children, experts, and amateur science buffs. The topics of their conversations range from the science of cooking to the multiverse and string theory.

NOTES: _____

LAST OF THE SANDWALKERS, BY JAY HOSLER (2015) SCIENCE
GRAPHIC NOVEL [2]
AGE RANGE 10 AND UP / GRADE LEVEL 5 AND UP / THEME:
ENTOMOLOGY, BEETLES

Nestled in the grass under the big palm tree by the edge of the
desert there is an entire civilization—a civilization of beetles. In this
bug's paradise, beetles write books, run restaurants, and even do
scientific research. But not too much scientific research is allowed
by the powerful elders. Lucy is not one to quietly cooperate, however. This tiny field scientist defies the law of her safe but authoritarian
home and leads a team of researchers out into the desert. Their
mission is to discover something about the greater world but what
lies in wait for them is going to change everything Lucy thought she
knew.

Jay Hosler is a biology professor and a cartoonist.

NOTES: _____

NEUROCOMIC, BY HANA ROŠ, ILLUSTRATED BY MATTEO
FARINELLA (2013) GRAPHIC NOVEL [4]
AN ADULT BOOK SUITABLE FOR YOUNG ADULT READERS. / THEME:
NEUROSCIENCE, BRAIN

Neurocomic is a fascinating and very readable journey through the
human brain. Along the way, you'll encounter neuron forests, memory caves, enlightening insights and great pioneers of neuroscience.

Hana Roš, PhD, is a neuroscientist from Oxford University, England.
Matteo Farinella, PhD, is an illustrator specializing in graphic journal-
ism and scientific illustration.

NOTES: _____

**PRIMATES, FEARLESS SCIENCE OF JANE GOODALL,
DIAN FOSSEY, AND BIRUTE GALDIKAS,** BY JIM OTTAVIANI
(2011) TRUE STORY A NONFICTION GRAPHIC NOVEL [3]
AGE RANGE 12 – 18 / GRADE LEVEL 7 – 9 / THEME: PRIMATE
RESEARCH

Compresses the fascinating stories of three groundbreaking scientists—Jane Goodall, Dian Fossey, and Biruté Galdikas—into a slim
graphic novel without skimping on their characters and discoveries.

NOTES: _____

SCIENCE: A DISCOVERY IN COMICS, BY MARGREET DE HEER
(2012) NONFICTION GRAPHIC NOVEL [4]
AGE RANGE 9-12 / GRADE LEVEL 4-7 / THEME: SCIENCE CONCEPTS

Explaining different scientific disciplines in clear, colorful chapters, this illustrated presentation is a great way to introduce young readers to a complex topic. This is not a story in the strict sense but In her easily accessible style, Margreet de Heer visualizes science and has created a book that is fun and approachable reading.

NOTES: _____

SECRET SCIENCE ALLIANCE AND THE COPYCAT CROOK,
BY ELEANOR DAVIS, THE: (2009) GRAPHIC NOVEL [2]
AGE RANGE 10-13 / GRADE LEVEL 3-7 / THEME: SCIENCE, INVENTION, ADVENTURE

Julian Calendar is 11 and is a smart transfer student trying to fit in at his new middle school. He discovers two other smart kids and together they form the Secret Science Alliance. They create a book of blueprints for such cunning creations as the stinkometer, sticky and dangerous gluebombs, and the flying Kablovsky Copter. However, their blueprints are stolen by the evil Dr. Stringer who has plans for them.

NOTES: _____

T-MINUS: THE RACE TO THE MOON, BY JIM OTTAVIANI (2009)
TRUE STORY, GRAPHIC NOVEL [3]
AGE RANGE 13 AND UP / GRADE LEVEL 7 AND UP TO ADULT/ THEME: SPACE, MOON LANDING

This lightly fictionalized but largely true graphic novel tracks the exciting story of two world superpowers racing to land a man on the moon and the dedicated scientists who made the dream a reality. Loaded with technical information on the particulars of rocketry and space flight the story unfolds through the eyes of the figures working behind the scenes to make this miracle happen.

NOTES: _____

POETRY BOOKS OF NATURE AND SCIENCE

Ages 4 and up; includes poems written by famous poets as well as poetry by other poets and by science educators

_____ *Brain Juice: Science, Fresh Squeezed!,* by Carol Diggery Shields

_____ *Creatures of Earth, Sea, and Sky,* by Georgia Heard

_____ *Earth, My Likeness: Nature Poetry of Walt Whitman,* by Howard Nelson, Editor

_____ *National Geographic Book of Animal Poetry,* by Patrick Lewis, Editor

_____ *National Geographic Book of Nature Poetry,* by Patrick Lewis,

_____ *Poetry for Young People–Robert Frost,* by Gary D. Schmidt, Editor

_____ *Poetry of Science, The,* compiled by Sylvia Vardell and Janet Wong

_____ *Robert Frost – Stopping by Woods On A Snowy Evening,* by Robert Frost

_____ *Spectacular Science,* selected by Lee Bennett Hopkins

_____ *Tree That Time Built, The, A Celebration of Nature, Science, and Imagination,* by Mary Ann Hoberman and Linda Winston

Descriptions For Science Poetry Books

BRAIN JUICE: SCIENCE, FRESH SQUEEZED!, BY CAROL DIGGERY SHIELDS (2003)
AGE RANGE 10-13 / GRADE LEVEL 4-7 / THEME: POETRY OF SCIENCE

The 41 poems in *Brain Juice: Science, Fresh Squeezed!* Illustrated by cartoonist Richard Thompson, distill scientific facts into clever rhymes and mnemonics. In the tragic romance, "Chemical Reaction," Shields writes, "He was acid, she was alkaline. He wasn't her type, but he thought she looked fine." Thompson's drawings combine with the text to saturate the pages with wit and levity.

NOTES: _____

CREATURES OF EARTH, SEA, AND SKY, BY GEORGIA HEARD (1992)
AGE RANGE 9-12 / GRADE LEVEL 4-6 / THEME: POETRY OF SCIENCE

Creatures of land, water, and sky are featured here in short poems for early readers. Poet and educator Georgia Heard writes about humming birds and eagles, whales and dolphins, elephants and snakes. Naturalist and illustrator Jennifer Dewey captures each animal in dramatic detail. The slim book is written and illustrated with a reverence for the natural world and for wildlife.

NOTES: _____

EARTH, MY LIKENESS: NATURE POETRY OF WALT WHITMAN, BY HOWARD NELSON, EDITOR (2006)
AGE RANGE YOUNG ADULT AND ADULT / GRADE 9 AND UP / THEME: NATURE POETRY

This collection of Walt Whitman's nature poems is beautifully illustrated with art by Roderick MacIver. Nelson has written a thoughtful Introduction that perhaps will only be read by older teens, and the adults who are its anticipated audience. The selection of poems however is very suitable for young adults from about age 14 years.

NOTES: _____

NATIONAL GEOGRAPHIC BOOK OF ANIMAL POETRY, BY PATRICK LEWIS, EDITOR (2012)
AGE RANGE ALL AGES THROUGH ADULT, GRADE ALL AND ADULT / THEME: ANIMAL POETRY WITH PHOTOGRAPHS

This is a large-format book suitable for the whole family. Patrick Lewis has selected 200 poems by such poets as Robert Frost, Emily Dickinson and more, and illustrated them with amazing National Geographic photographs. A useful set of indices make it possible to find poems by author, title, first line or subject.

NOTES: _____

NATIONAL GEOGRAPHIC BOOK OF NATURE POETRY, BY PATRICK LEWIS, EDITOR (2015)
AGE RANGE ALL AGES AND ADULT, GRADE LEVEL ALL AND ADULT / THEME: NATURE POETRY WITH PHOTOGRAPHS

This assortment of nature-themed verse is breathtaking. The poem selections represent a variety of styles, time periods, countries of origin, lengths, and themes; all are set against a visually stunning backdrop of full-bleed photographs. The collection contains poems by well known poets as well as lesser known ones.

NOTES: _____

POETRY FOR YOUNG PEOPLE–ROBERT FROST, BY GARY D. SCHMIDT, EDITOR (1994)
AGE RANGE 10 UP / GRADE LEVEL 6 UP / THEME: NATURAL SCIENCE POETRY

This is a visually appealing, slim book of 41 of Frost's poems selected by Schmidt. It is arranged by the seasons and has fine, specially commissioned illustrations by Henri Sorenson. The selection is targeted for young people but the poems are ageless and the book will be enjoyed by adults too.

NOTES: _____

POETRY OF SCIENCE, THE, COMPILED BY SYLVIA VARDELL AND JANET WONG (2015)
AGE RANGE 10 UP / GRADE LEVEL 6 UP / THEME: SCIENCE POETRY

This large-format, book has 248 poems by 78 poets about science, technology, engineering, math, animals, plants, machines, earth and space, scientists and more. The illustrations are engaging line drawings that do not overwhelm the easy-to-read text. There is a teacher edition of this book.

NOTES: _____

ROBERT FROST – STOPPING BY WOODS ON A SNOWY EVENING, BY ROBERT FROST, ILLUSTRATED BY SUSAN JEFFERS (1978)
AGE RANGE 4-8 / GRADE LEVEL PREK-3 / THEME: NATURE POETRY

This simple slim volume beautifully illustrates a single Frost poem that is an enduring favorite. Susan Jeffers has detail and subtle color to her sweeping, soft backgrounds of frosty New England scenes. There are animals to find among the trees, and the kindly figure with his "promises to keep" exudes warmth as he stops to appreciate the quiet delights of winter.

NOTES: _____

SPECTACULAR SCIENCE, SELECTED BY LEE BENNETT HOPKINS (1999)
AGE RANGE 5 UP / GRADE LEVEL K-3 / THEME POETRY OF SCIENCE

A collection of 15 colorfully illustrated poems exploring interesting scientific events and topics, such as weather and the process of freezing. The collection includes poems by Valerie Worth, Lilian Moore, Carl Sandburg, David McCord, and Alice Schertle and offers an invitation to ponder what science is and what scientists do.

NOTES: _____

TREE THAT TIME BUILT, THE A CELEBRATION OF NATURE, SCIENCE, AND IMAGINATION, SELECTED BY MARY ANN HOBERMAN AND LINDA WINSTON (2009)
AGE RANGE 9 AND UP / GRADE LEVEL 7 AND UP / THEME: POETRY OF SCIENCE

A fine book of poetry for all ages with more than 100 poems celebrating nature, science, and the environment, selected by the Children's Poet Laureate. With a focus on the outdoors, the collection taps into today's environmental movement. Included is an exclusive audio CD of many of the poets reading their own work. The collection showcases a wide range of poets, including: Theodore Roethke, Dylan Thomas, Carl Sandburg, Douglas Florian, Jeff Moss, Jack Prelutsky, and Mary Ann Hoberman.

NOTES: _____

PLAY SCRIPTS WITH SCIENCE AS PART OF THE PLOT

Ages 14 and up; plays that address science information and issues and are professionally performed for the general public.

_____ **Arcadia,** by Tom Stoppard (1973) Play script, Fiction

_____ **Constellations,** by Nick Payne (2012) Play script, Fiction

_____ **Copenhagen,** by Michael Frayn (1998) Play script, Fact-based fiction

_____ **Enemy | Flint,** by Diana Burbano (2017) Fact-based fiction

_____ **Farnsworth Invention, The,** by Aaron Sorkin (2007) Play script, Fact-based fiction

_____ **On The Verge,** by Eric Overmeyer (1985) Play script, comedy fiction, time travel

_____ **Photograph 51,** by Anna Ziegler (2015) Play script, Fact-based fiction

_____ **Proof,** by David Auburn, (2000) Play script, Fiction

_____ **QED,** by Peter Parnell, (2001) Play script, fact based fiction

_____ **Tooth and Claw,** by Michael Hollinger (2010) Play script, Fiction

Descriptions for Science Play Scripts

ARCADIA, BY TOM STOPPARD (1973) FICTION, PLAY SCRIPT [4]
AN ADULT PLAY SUITABLE FOR INTERESTED READERS OF 15 AND UP
THEME: MATHEMATICS

The play opens in 1809 where the daughter of a landed gentry family, Thomasina Coverley, is being tutored by the handsome Septimus Hodge who wants her to concentrate on Fermat's last theorem. In the course of the play algebra and algorithms, and fashions in garden design are examined while the play explores the nature of truth and time between centuries.

NOTES: _____

CONSTELLATIONS, BY NICK PAYNE (2012)
FICTION PLAY SCRIPT [4]
AN ADULT PLAY SUITABLE FOR INTERESTED READERS OF 15 AND UP
THEME: PHYSICS

A play about Marianne, a physicist, and Roland, a beekeeper; about free will, friendship, and traditional romance that collides with quantum mechanics and relativity.

NOTES: _____

COPENHAGEN, BY MICHAEL FRAYN (1998)
FACT-BASED FICTION, PLAY SCRIPT [4]
AN ADULT PLAY SUITABLE FOR INTERESTED READERS OF 15 AND UP
THEME: PHYSICS, FISSION

This play is based on an after-their-deaths meeting between the physicists Niels Bohr and Werner Heisenberger that occurred in Copenhagen in 1941. The plot portrays the conflict of scientists' curiosity versus conscience – specifically in regard to the building of the first atomic bomb. The play script is somewhat complex and is recommended for those with an existing understanding of the topic.

NOTES: _____

ENEMY | FLINT, BY DIANA BURBANO (2017)
FACT-BASED FICTION, PLAY SCRIPT [4]
ADULT AND YOUNG ADULT / THEME: WATER CONTAMINATION

Thia Stockmann, a bright young medical student, has discovered her town water supply has been poisoned. Her data, her personality and her determination offend first her family, then the town council, then the community but she becomes even more committed to doing what is right. Diana Burbano, a Colombian immigrant, is an Equity actor, and a playwright. Burbano's play is based on *An Enemy of the People* by Hedrick Ibsen and is suitable for high school and older.

NOTES: _____

FARNSWORTH INVENTION, THE, BY AARON SORKIN (2007)
FICTION BASED ON FACT, PLAY SCRIPT, [4]
AN ADULT PLAY SUITABLE FOR INTERESTED READERS OF 15 AND UP
THEME: INVENTION

It's 1929. Two ambitious visionaries race against each other to invent a device called "television." Separated by two thousand miles, each knows that if he stops working, even for a moment, the other will gain the edge. Who will unlock the key to the greatest innovation of the 20th century: the ruthless media mogul, or the self-taught Idaho farm boy?

NOTES: _____

ON THE VERGE, BY ERIC OVERMEYER (1985)
COMEDY FICTION, TIME TRAVEL, PLAY SCRIPT [4]
AN ADULT PLAY SUITABLE FOR YOUNG ADULT AUDIENCES 15 AND UP / THEME: EXPLORATION

A jaunt through a continuum of space, time, history, geography, feminism and fashion. The year is 1888 when Mary, Fanny, and Alex, three women who are each intrepid world explorers in their own right, band together to conquer 'Terra Incognita', the last and most mysterious of unexplored territories.

NOTES: _____

PHOTOGRAPH 51, BY ANNA ZIEGLER (2015)
FICTION BASED ON FACT, PLAY SCRIPT, [4]
AN ADULT PLAY SUITABLE FOR YOUNG ADULT AUDIENCES 15 AND
UP / THEME: DNA, FRANKLIN

This very short book, the script for Ziegler's one act play, tells the story of how Franklin, Wilkins, Crick, and Watson discovered the structure of DNA. The plot focuses on the often-overlooked role of x-ray crystallographer Rosalind Franklin in the discovery of the double helix structure of DNA. Each scene provides banter, some-times funny, sometimes sad or informative.

NOTES: _____

PROOF, BY DAVID AUBURN, (2000) FICTION, PLAY SCRIPT, [4]
AN ADULT PLAY SUITABLE FOR INTERESTED READERS OF 15 AND UP
/ MENTAL STABILITY, MATHEMATICS,

Proof is about scientists whose science matters less than their humanity. It is about a struggle with mathematical genius and mental illness and the search for the truth behind a mysterious mathematical proof concerning prime numbers.

The play won the 2001 Pulitzer Prize for Drama and Tony Award for Best Play.

NOTES: _____

QED, BY PETER PARNELL, (2001)
FICTION BASED ON FACTS, PLAY SCRIPT [4]
AN ADULT PLAY SUITABLE FOR INTERESTED READERS OF 15 AND UP
/ THEME: PHYSICS

The play is set in 1986 in the office of the famous, Nobel Prize winning modern physicist, Richard Feynman, at the California Institute of Technology in Pasadena.

Feynman is preparing to play the bongo drums in a stage perfor-mance; working on a lecture; fielding phone calls from students, visiting Russians, doctors with ominous news about his spreading cancer; and, is enjoying an unscheduled visit from a beautiful girl who shares his passion for physics, music and the joy of living.

NOTES: _____

TOOTH AND CLAW, BY MICHAEL HOLLINGER (2010) FICTION,
PLAY-SCRIPT [4]
AN ADULT PLAY SUITABLE FOR INTERESTED READERS OF 15 AND UP
THEME: ECOSYSTEMS

In Michael Hollinger's *Tooth and Claw*, reptile specialist Schuyler
Baines-"the savior of giant tortoises" and the first female director of
the Charles Darwin Research Station-arrives in Galapagos full of
ideas and idealism. But when she becomes aware of an exploding
black market that threatens to destroy the islands' fragile ecosystem,
Schuyler shuts the industry down, sparking a deadly, survival-of-the-
fittest conflict with native fishermen.
NOTES: _____

Take Off with Books

-BY OGDEN NASH

Take off with books,
Not with the rockets roar,
Take off in silence
And in fancy soar
At rocket speed
To every land and time,
And see, spread out beneath,
Past, present, future as you higher climb.
No path forbid, no darkling secret hid;
Books reached the moon before real rockets did.

KIDS' SCIENCE MAGAZINES

Kids' Magazines Featuring Nature and Science

Age Range 3 through 14 years

*Most of these magazines have a print-version option.
Some may be only online.*

ASK, FOR AGES 7-10 (HTTP://CRICKETMEDIA.COM/COMPANY)

ASK is promoted as "the best magazine for children who like to ask lots of questions," The magazine is filled with fun and fascinating facts, informative scientific articles, and hands-on activities. Emphasis is on science, but the magazine does not lose sight of science's daily application to the arts. There are no advertisements. (Print and online versions.)

NOTES: _____

CLICK, FOR AGES 3-6 (HTTP://CRICKETMEDIA.COM/COMPANY)

Fostering curiosity and a sense of inquiry each issue explores a single subject from varied angles through real-life photographs, cartoon art, fact-based storytelling, experiments, and activities, Recent subjects included skin–how various animals shed theirs or change colors, how touch receptors work in humans, what it's like to read and write in Braille, and how plants protect themselves. (Print and online versions.)

NOTES: _____

CRICKET, FOR AGES 9-14 (HTTP://CRICKETMEDIA.COM/COMPANY)

This is an exceptional literary magazine that includes science amongst its wide-ranging article topics. It includes fiction, nonfiction, poetry and art. *Cricket* stories are often serialized, giving readers engaging substance. Recent nonfiction pieces explored the roots of an Irish legend, the fascinating ruby-throated hummingbird, the hard lives of 18th century chimney sweeps, and the accomplishments of a busy horror actor and a pioneering female acrobatic swimmer. (Print and online versions.)

NOTES: _____

KAZOO, FOR AGES 5-10
(HTTP://WWW.KAZOOMAGAZINE.COM/ABOUT/)

Kazoo premiered in 2016 and describes itself as is a new kind of quarterly print magazine for girls It features stories on art, nature, science, tinkering and tech, and critical thinking. In past issues Ornithologist Amanda Rodewald, Ph.D., Director of Conservation Science at the Cornell Lab of Ornithology led readers on a bird-themed scavenger hunt; Aerospace Engineer Ella Atkins, Ph.D., of the University of Michigan explained the principles behind five different DIY flying gizmos, including a napkin parachute, a paper helicopter, a balloon hovercraft, a pyramid kite and a paper airplane. (Print version only)

NOTES: _____

MUSE, FOR AGES 9-14 (HTTP://CRICKETMEDIA.COM/COMPANY)

MUSE, published nine times a year is the science and arts magazine for kids. It includes articles on various topics written by award-winning authors and accompanied by high-quality illustration and photography. Past issues have included articles about vegetarianism, extraterrestrial life, naked mole-rats, the origin of the moon, and insects. *MUSE* is a good replacement for kids who are outgrowing *ASK* magazine and are interested in science, history, and the arts. (Print and online versions.)

NOTES: _____

NATIONAL GEOGRAPHIC KIDS, FOR 6 AND UP & NATIONAL GEOGRAPHIC LITTLE KIDS --FOR 3-6   (HTTPS://SHOP. NATIONALGEOGRAPHIC.COM/COLLECTIONS/MAGAZINES)

Each issue is packed with stories and fine photography about wildlife, science, technology, popular culture, and more. The articles are designed to keep kids reading, thinking, learning and having fun! (Print and online versions)

NOTES: _____

OWL, FOR AGES 9-13
(HTTP://WWW.OWLKIDS.COM/MAGAZINES/OWL/)

OWL highlights elements of science, technology, engineering, art, and math to encourage kids to discover, explore, engage, and inspire. Issues include cool tech news, expert interviews, ground-breaking discoveries and innovations, futuristic inventions and hands-on-building, book and movie reviews, reader art and advice, contests and more. *ChickaDee* (http://www.owlkids.com/magazines/chickadee/) published by the same company has a similar focus for the 6-9 age range. (Print and online versions)

NOTES: _____

RANGER RICK, FOR AGES 7-12 AND RANGER RICK JR, FOR AGES 4-7 (HTTPS://RANGERRICK.ORG) AND (HTTPS://RANGERRICK.ORG/MAGAZINES/RANGER-RICK-JR/)

These are children's nature magazines published by the United States National Wildlife Federation. The magazines offer feature articles and activities in order to spark interest in the outdoors and encourage involvement in caring for the environment. The maga-zine's primary intention is to instill a passion for nature and promote activity outdoors. (Print and online versions)

NOTES: _____

WHIZZ POP BANG, FOR AGES 6-12
 (HTTPS://WWW.WHIZZPOPBANG.COM)

WHIZZ POP BANG is an award-winning, gender neutral, children's online science magazine originating in the UK. It makes science fun and engaging. Each month's magazine is bursting with facts, hands-on experiments, science news and discoveries, as well as interviews with real scientists. (Online only)

NOTES: _____

ZOOBOOKS, FOR AGES 6-12 (HTTP://WWW.ZOOBOOKS.COM)

Each magazine explores the anatomy, habitat, socialization, and ecological role of a single animal or animal group. *Zoobooks* is now part of the National Wildlife Federation's Ranger Rick team. (Print and online versions)

NOTES: _____

Index of Titles

___ *Book Scavenger, The,* by Jennifer Chambliss Bertman — Fiction [3]

___ *Born Free,* by Joy Adamson — True Story [3]

___ *Boy Who Harnessed The Wind, The: Young Readers' Edition,* by William Kamkwamba — True Story [2]

___ *Brain Juice: Science, Fresh Squeezed,* by Carol Diggery Shields — Poetry

___ *Brilliant Fall of Gianna Z., The,* by Kate Messner — Fiction [2]

___ *Case of the Missing Moonstone, The (The Wollstonecraft Detective Agency, Book 1),* by Jordan Stratford — Fiction [3]

___ *Certain Ambiguity, A: A Mathematical Novel,* by Gaurav Suri and Hartosh Bal — Fiction [4)

___ *Charles Darwin's On the Origin of Species; A Graphic Adaptation,* by Michael Keller — Graphic Novel [4]

___ *Charlie's Raven,* by Jean Craighead George — Nature Fiction [3]

___ *Charlotte's Web,* by E.B. White — Fiction [2]

___ *Clan Apis,* by Jay Hosler — Nonfiction Graphic Novel [3]

___ *Chasing Vermeer,* by Blue Balliett — Fiction [3]

___ *Clockwork or All Wound Up,* by Philip Pullman — Fantasy Fiction [2]

___ *Constellations,* by Nick Payne — Play Script, Fiction [4]

___ *Copenhagen,* by Michael Frayn — Play Script, Fact-based Fiction [4]

___ *Countdown Conspiracy, The,* by Katie Slivensky — Mystery Fiction [2]

___ *Creatures of Earth, Sea, and Sky,* by Georgia Heard — Poetry

___ *Curious Garden The,* by Peter Brown — Fiction [1]

___ *Dear Greenpeace,* by Simon James — Fiction Picture Book [1]

___ *Dialogues, The,* by Clifford Johnson — Graphic Novel [4]

___ *Dinosaur Hunters,* by Catherine Chambers — Fiction [2]

___ *Dinosaurs Before Dark,* by Mary Pope Osborne — Fiction [2]

___ *Double Helix, The,* by James D. Watson — Nonfiction [4]

___ *Dragon Bones and Dinosaur Eggs,* by Ann Bausum — True Story [3]

Lucy Hawking — Adventure Fiction [2]

___ *Girls Who Looked Under Rocks,* by Jeanine Atkins and Paula Conner — True Stories [2]

___ *Great Trouble, The: A Mystery of London, the Blue Death, and a Boy Called Eel,* by Deborah Hopkinson — Narrative Nonfiction Novel [3]

___ *Hatchet,* by Gary Paulsen — Fiction Survival Story [3]

___ *Hidden Figures,* by Margot Lee Shetterly — Fact-based Fiction [4]

___ *Hoot,* by Carl Hiassen — Ecological Mystery Fiction [3]

___ *House of the Scorpion, The,* by Nancy Farmer — Science Fiction [3]

___ *Humblebee Hunter, The,* by Deborah Hopkinson — Fiction [1]

___ *In The Shadow of Man,* by Jane Goodall — True Story, Personal Narrative [3]

___ *Isaac The Alchemist: Secrets of Isaac Newton, Reveal'd,* by Mary Losure — Narrative Nonfiction [3]

___ *Island of the Blue Dolphins,* by Scott O'Dell — True Story Novel [3]

___ *Island of the Unknowns: A Mystery,* by Benedict Carey — Fiction [3]

___ *Itch,* by Simon Mayo — Adventure Fiction [2]

___ *Jack and the Geniuses, At the Bottom of the World,* by Bill Nye and Gregory Mone — Adventure Fiction [3]

___ *Joan Procter, Dragon Doctor: The Woman Who Loved Reptiles,* by Patricia Valdez — Biography [1]

___ *Julie of the Wolves,* by Jean Craighead George — Nature Fiction [3]

___ *Kine,* by A. R. Lloyd — Fiction [3]

___ *King Solomon's Ring,* by Konrad Lorenz — Behavioral Science Nonfiction [4]

___ *Lab Girl,* by Hope Jahren — Autobiographical True Story [4]

___ *Last Days of Night, The,* by Graham Moore — Narrative Nonfiction [4]

___ *Last of the Sandwalkers,* by Jay Hosler — Nonfiction Graphic Novel [2]

___ *National Geographic Book of Nature Poetry,* by Patrick Lewis, Editor — Poetry

___ *Nefertiti, the Spidernaut: The Jumping Spider Who Learned to Hunt in Space,* by Darcy Patterson — Nonfiction [2]

___ *Neurocomic,* by Hana Ros, illustrated by Matteo Farinella — Graphic Novel [4]

___ *Never Cry Wolf,* by Farley Mowat — True Story [3]

___ *New World of Mr. Tompkins, The,* by George Gamow and Russell Stannard — Fiction [3]

___ *On a Beam of Light: A Story of Albert Einstein,* by Jennifer Berne — Biography [1]

___ *On The Verge,* by Eric Overmeyer — Play Script, Comedy Fiction, Time Travel [4]

___ *One and Only Ivan, The,* by Katherine Applegate — Fiction [2]

___ *Orcas Around Me,* by Debra Page — Fact-based fiction [1].

___ *Outside Your Window: A First Book of Nature,* by Nicola Davies — Picture Storybook [1]

___ *Over and Under the Snow,* by Kate Messner — Picture Storybook [1]

___ *Passion for Science, A,* by Lewis Wolpert and Alison Richards — Nonfiction [4]

___ *Pax,* by Sara Pennypacker — Fiction [3]

___ *Petroplague,* by Amy Rogers — Fiction [4]

___ *Phantom Tollbooth, The,* by Norton Juster — Fantasy Fiction [3]

___ *Photograph 51 by,* Anna Ziegler — Play Script, Fact-based Fiction [4]

___ *Poetry for Young People—Robert Frost,* by Gary D. Schmidt, Editor — Poetry

___ *Poetry of Science, The,* compiled by Sylvia Vardell and Janet Wong — Poetry

___ *Practice Effect, The,* by David Brin — Science Fiction [4]

___ *Primates, Fearless Science,* of Jane Goodall, Dian Fossey, and Birute Galdikas by Jim Ottaviani — True Story, Graphic Novel [3]

___ *Privileged Hands: A Scientific Life,* by Geerat Vermeij — Autobiography [3]

___ *Silverwing,* by Kenneth Oppel — Nature Fiction [2]

___ *Snowflake Bentley,* by Jacqueline Briggs Martin — Fact-based Fiction [1]

___ *Spectacular Science,* selected by Lee Bennett Hopkins — Poetry

___ *Story of Charlotte's Web,* by Michael Sims — True Story Nonfiction [4]

___ *Stuart Little,* by E.B. White — Fiction [2]

___ *Summer of the Monkeys,* by Wilson Rawls — Adventure Fiction [2]

___ *Swallows and Amazons,* by Arthur Ransome — Fiction [2]

___ *Sweetness at the Bottom of the Pie, The,* by Alan Bradley — Mystery Fiction [3]

___ *T-Minus: The Race to the Moon,* by Jim Ottaviani — True Story, Graphic Novel [3]

___ *Tales from Watership Down,* by Richard Adams — Fiction [3]

___ *There's a Hair in My Dirt,* by Gary Larson — Fiction [3]

___ *Time and Space of Uncle Albert, The,* by Russell Stannard — Fiction [3]

___ *Time,* by Roger Reid — Adventure Fiction [2]

___ *Tin Snail, The,* by Cameron McAllister — Fiction [2]

___ *Tom's Midnight Garden,* by Philippa Pearce — Fantasy Fiction [2]

___ *Tooth and Claw,* by Michael Hollinger — Play Script, Fiction [4]

___ *Town Secrets,* (The Book of Adam 1), by Scott Gelowitz — Fiction [3]

___ *Treasure (Seed Savers Book 1),* by S. Smith — Fiction [2]

___ *Tree That Time Built, The, A Celebration of Nature, Science, and Imagination,* by Mary Ann Hoberman — Poetry

___ *Tricking the Tallyman,* by Jacqueline Davies — Fiction [2]

___ *Trumpet of the Swan,* by E.B. White — Fiction [2]

___ *Turtle, Turtle, Watch Out!,* by April Pulley Sayre — Fiction, Picture Storybook [1]

___ *Uncle Tungsten,* by Oliver Sacks — Memoir [4]

___ *Under the Egg,* by Laura Marx Fitzgerald — Fiction [3]

Index of Story Book and Novel Authors

Beaty, Andrea & Roberts, David, *Ada Twist Scientist*

Beaty, Andrea & Roberts, David, *Rosie Revere, Engineer*

Berne, Jennifer, *On a Beam of Light: A Story of Albert Einstein]*

Bertman, Jennifer Chambliss, *The Book Scavenger, The*

Bradley, Alan, *The Sweetness at the Bottom of the Pie*

Brin, David, *The Practice Effect*

Brown, Peter, *The Curious Garden,*

Brown, Peter, *The Wild Robot*

Don Brown, *Rare Treasure: Mary Anning and Her Remarkable Discoveries*

Brown, Shannon, *The Feather Chase*

Burns, Loree, *Life on Surtsey: Iceland's Upstart Island*

Cameron, Eleanor, *The Wonderful Flight to the Mushroom Planet*

Cary, Benedict, *Island of the Unknowns: A Mystery*

Chambers, Catherine, *Dinosaur Hunters*

Cousteau, Philippe, *Follow the Moon Home: A Tale of One Idea, Twenty Kids, and a Hundred Sea Turtles (with Deborah Hopkinson)*

Crew, Megan, *The Way We Fall by Megan Crew*

Dahl, Roald, *Matilda*

Davis, Eleanor, *The Secret Science Alliance and the Copycat Crook*

Davies, Jacqueline, *Tricking the Tallyman*

Davies, Nicola, *Outside Your Window: A First Book of Nature*

de Heer, Margreet, *Science: A Discovery in Comics*

de Kruif, Paul, *Microbe Hunters*

Doerr, Anthony, *The Shell Collector*

Durrell, Gerald, My Family and Other Animals

Engle, Margarita, *Flying Girl, The: How Aida de Acosta Learned to Soar*

Farmer, Nancy, *The House of the Scorpion*

Fitzgerald, Laura Marx, *Under the Egg*

Fleischman, Paul, *Seedfolks*

Gamow, Igor, *The Adventures of Mr. Thompkins, Volume 1*

Gamow, George and Russell Stannard, *The New World of Mr. Tompkins*

Gelowitz, Scott, *Town Secrets (The Book of Adam 1)*

George, Jean Craighead, *Water Sky*

George, Jean Craighead, *Charlie's Raven*

George, Jean Craighead, *Julie of the Wolves*

George, Jean Craighead, *My Side of the Mountain*

George, Jean Craighead, *Who Really Killed Cock Robin?*

Gilmore, Robert, *The Wizard of Quarks*

Glynn, Jenifer, *My Sister Rosalind Franklin: A Family Memoir*

Goodall, Jane, *In The Shadow of Man*

Grabenstein, Chris, *Escape from Mr. Lemoncello's Library*

Green, John, *An Abundance of Katherines*

Hawking, Stephen and Lucy Hawking, *George's Secret Key to the Universe*

Herriot, James, *Every Living Thing*

Hiassen, Carl, *Hoot*

Hickam, Homer, *Rocket Boys*

Holm, Jennifer, *The Fourteenth Goldfish*

Holt, Nathalia, *Rise of the Rocket Girls*

Hopinson, Deborah, *Great Trouble, The: A Mystery of London, the Blue Death, and a Boy Called Eel*

Hopkinson, Deborah, *Humblebee Hunter, The by Deborah Hopkinson*

Hosler, Jay, *Clan Apis*

Hosler, Jay, *Last of the Sandwalkers*

Isdell, Wendy, *A Gebra Named Al*

Jahren, Hope, *Lab Girl*

James, Simon, *Dear Greenpeace*

James, Simon, *The Wild Woods*

Johnson, Clifford, *The Dialogues*

Johnston, Tony, *Winter is Coming*

Juster, Norton, *The Phantom Tollbooth*

Kamkwamba, William, *The Boy Who Harnessed The Wind: Young Readers' Edition*

Keating, Jess, *Shark Lady*

Kehoe, Tim, *Vincent Shadow: Toy Inventor*

Keller, Michael, *Charles Darwin's On the Origin of Species; A Graphic Adaptation*

Kelly, Jacqueline, *The Evolution of Calpurnia Tate*

Kelly, Scott, *My Journey to the Stars*

Kemp, J.G. *Mary Andromeda and the Amazing Eye*

Kjorness, Chris and Jenny, *The Moon is Made of Cheese*

L'Engle, Madeline, *A Wrinkle in Time*

Larson, Gary, *There's a Hair in My Dirt*

Leonard, M.G., *Beetle Boy*

Lewis, Gill, *Wild Wings*

Lloyd, A.R., *Kine*

Lorenz, Konrad, *King Solomon's Ring*

Lorenz, Konrad, *Man Meets Dog*

Losure, Mary, *Isaac The Alchemist: Secrets of Isaac Newton, Reveal'd*

Mandeville, Chris, *Seeds: a post-apocalyptic adventure*

Martin, Jacqueline Briggs, *Snowflake Bentley*

Mayo, Simon, *Itch*

McAllister, Cameron, *The Tin Snail*

McAnuity, Stacy, *The Miscalculations of Lightning Girl*

McNeil, Gretchen, *3:59*

Messner, Kate, *Eye of the Storm*

Messner, Kate, *The Brilliant Fall of Gianna Z.*

Messner, Kate, *Over and Under the Snow*

Moore, Graham, *The Last Days of Night*

Moorhouse, Tom, *River Singers, The*

Mowat, Farley, *Boat Who Wouldn't Float, The*

Mowat, Farley, *Never Cry Wolf*

Mullin, Mike, *Ashfall*

Newman, Patricia, *Sea Otter Heroes: The Predators That Saved an Ecosystem*

Nidever, R.C., *Finding the Lone Woman of San Nicolas Island.*

Nye, Bill and Gregory Mone, *Jack and the Geniuses, At the Bottom of the World*

O'Brien, Robert C., *Mrs. Frisby and the Rats of NIMH*

O'Dell, Scott, *Island of the Blue Dolphins*

Oppel, Kenneth, *Airborn*

Oppel, Kenneth, *Silverwing*

Osborne, Mary Pope, *Dinosaurs Before Dark*

Ottaviani, Jim, *Primates, Fearless Science of Jane Goodall, Dian Fossey, and Birute Galdikas*

Ottaviani, Jim, *T-Minus: The Race to the Moon*

Page, Debra, *Orcas Around Me*

Park, Linda Sue, *Project Mulberry Park*

Patterson, Darcy, *Nefertiti, the Spidernaut: The Jumping Spider Who Learned to Hunt in Space*

Pattison, Darcy, *Wisdom, the Midway Albatross*

Paulsen, Gary, *Hatchet*

Pearce, Philippa, *Tom's Midnight Garden*

Pennypacker, Sara, *Pax*

Pettanati, Jeanne, *Galileo's Journal: 1609-1610*

Pfeffer, Susan Beth, *Life as We Knew It*

Ponder, A.J., *Frankie Files, The*

Pullman, Philip, *Clockwork or All Wound Up*

Pullman, Philip, *The Firework Maker's Daughter*

Pullman, Philip, *The Scarecrow and his Servant*

Ransome, Arthur, *Swallows and Amazons*

Raskin, Ellen, *Westing Game, The*

Rawls, Wilson, *Summer of the Monkeys*

Reid, Roger, *Longleaf*

Reid, Roger, *Time*

Rink, Paul, *Admiral Richard Byrd: Alone in the Antarctic*

Rinker, Sherri Duskey, *Mighty, Mighty Construction Site*

Robinson, Kim Stanley, *40 Signs of Rain*

Rogers, Amy, *Petroplague*

Ros, Hana, *Neurocomic by Hana Ros*

Sachar, Louis, *Fuzzy Mud*

Sacks, Oliver, *Uncle Tungsten*

Sayer, April Pulley, *Turtle, Turtle, Watch Out!*

Seuss, Theodore, *The Lorax*

Shetterly, Margot Lee, *Hidden Figures*

Silvey, Anita, *Untamed: The Wild Life of Jane Goodall Foreword by Jane Goodall*

Sims, Michael, *The Story of Charlotte's Web*

Slivensky, Katie, *The Countdown Conspiracy*

Smith, S., *Treasure (Seed Savers Book 1)*

Stanley, Diane, *Ada Lovelace, Poet of Science: The First Computer Programmer*

Stannard, Russel, *The Time and Space of Uncle Albert*

Stead, Rebecca, *When You Reach Me*

Stewart, Trenton Lee, *The Mysterious Benedict Society*

Stobel, Dava, *Galileo's Daughter*

Stone, Tanya Lee, *Who Says Women Can't Be Computer Programmers? The Story of Ada Lovelace*

Stratford, Jordan, *The Case of the Missing Moonstone (The Wollstonecraft Detective Agency, Book 1)*

Sullivan, Robert, *Rats*

Suri, Gaurav and Hartosh Bal, *A Certain Ambiguity*

Index of Overt or Integrated Topics

A. Biology Animals and Plants
B. Ecology, Environment, Earth Science
C. Math, Chemistry, Physics, Technology
D. Space, Time Travel, Science Fiction
E. Discovering, Inventing, Problem Solving
F. Adventuring, Exploring, Surviving

A.
Biology, Animals and Plants

Early Reader: Ages 5-8 – [1]

Agriculture	*A Weed Is a Flower: The Life of George Washington Carver,* by Aliki (1965) True Story [1]
Gardening	*Curious Garden, The,* by Peter Brown (2009) Fiction [1]
Natural History	*Outside Your Window: A First Book of Nature,* by Nicola Davies (2012) Picture Book [1]
Natural History	*Over and Under the Snow,* by Kate Messner (2011) Picture Storybook [1]
Ocean Animals	*Orcas Around Me,* by Debra Page and Leslie W. Bowman (1997) Fact-based Fiction [1]

Reptiles	**Joan Procter, Dragon Doctor: The Woman Who Loved Reptiles,** by Patricia Valdez (2018) Biography [1]
Sea Turtles	**Follow the Moon Home: A Tale of One Idea, Twenty Kids, and a Hundred Sea Turtles,** by Phillippe Cousteau and Deborah Hopkinson (2016) Fiction [1]
Sea Turtles	**Turtle, Turtle, Watch Out!,** by April Pulley Sayre (2000) Fiction, Picture Storybook [1]
Sharks	**Shark Lady: The True Story of How Eugenie Clark Became the Ocean's Most Fearless Scientist,** by Jess Keating (2017) Fact-based Fiction [1]

Intermediate Reader: Ages 8-12
Biology, Animals and Plants [2]

Animal Behavior	**Summer of the Monkeys,** by Wilson Rawls (1976) Fiction Novel [2]
Bats	**Silverwing,** by Kenneth Oppel (1997) Fiction Novel [2]
Beetles	**Beetle Boy,** by M G Leonard (2016) Fiction Novel [2]
Dinosaurs, Time Travel	**Dinosaur Hunters,** by Catherine Chambers (2014) Fiction [2]
Dinosaurs, Time Travel,	**Dinosaurs Before Dark,** by Mary Pope Osborne (1992) Fiction [2]
Dog	**Riptide,** by Frances Ward Weller (1996) Fact-based Fiction [2]
Gorillas	**One and Only Ivan, The,** by Katherine Applegate (2012) Fiction [2]
Mouse fiction	**Stuart Little,** by E.B. White (1954) Fiction Novel [2]
Nature	**Longleaf,** by Roger Reid (2006) Fiction Novel [2]

Birds, Osprey	**Wild Wings,** by Gill Lewis (2011) Fiction [2]
Problem solving	**Trumpet of the Swan, The,** by E.B. White (1970) Fiction Novel [2]
Spider, Fiction	**Charlotte's Web,** by E.B. White (1952) Fiction Novel [2]
Spider, Nonfiction	**Nefertiti, the Spidernaut: The Jumping Spider Who Learned to Hunt in Space,** by Darcy Patterson (2016) Nonfiction [2]
Seeds, Adventure	**Treasure (Seed Savers Book 1),** by S. Smith (2012) Fiction Novel [2]
Trees	**Brilliant Fall of Gianna Z., The,** by Kate Messner (2009) Fiction [2]

Proficient Reader: Ages 10-13
Biology, Animals and Plants [3]

Animals	**My Family and Other Animals,** by Gerald Durrell (1956) Autobiography [3]
Bees	**Clan Apis,** by Jay Hosler (2000) Nonfiction Graphic Novel [3]
Beetles	**Last of the Sandwalkers,** by Jay Hosler (2015) Science Graphic Novel [3]
Biotech, Cloning	**House of the Scorpion, The,** by Nancy Farmer (2002) Fiction Novel [3]
Biology Molluscs	**Privileged Hands: A Scientific Life,** by Geerat Vermeij (1996) Autobiography [3]
Birds	**Charlie's Raven,** by Jean Craighead George (1960) Fiction Novel [3]
Chimpanzees	**In The Shadow of Man,** by Jane Goodall (1971) True Story, Personal Narrative [3]
Chimpanzees	**Untamed: The Wild Life of Jane Goodall,** by Anita Silvey, Foreword by Jane Goodall (2015) Biography [3]

Chimpanzees	*Primates, Fearless Science of Jane Goodall, Dian Fossey, and Birute Galdikas,* by Jim Ottaviani (2011) True Story, Nonfiction Graphic Novel [3]
Dinosaurs,	*Dragon Bones and Dinosaur Eggs,* by Ann Bausum (2000) True Story [3]
Ecology	*There's a Hair in My Dirt,* by Gary Larson (1998) Fiction [3]
Foxes	*Pax,* by Sara Pennypacker (2016) Fiction Novel [3]
Gardening	*Seedfolks,* by Paul Fleischman (1997) Fiction [3]
Microbiology, Medical	*Great Trouble, The: A Mystery of London, the Blue Death, and a Boy Called Eel,* by Deborah Hopkinson (2013) Fiction, based on a real event. [3]
Microbiology, Medical	*Way We Fall, The* by Megan Crew (2012) Fiction [3]
Nature, Observing	*Evolution of Calpurnia Tate, The,* by Jacqueline Kelly (2009) Fiction [3]
Owls	*Hoot,* by Carl Hiassen (2002) Fiction Novel [3]
Rabbits	*Tales from Watership Down,* by Richard Adams (1996) Fiction [3]
Rats-fiction	*Mrs. Frisby and the Rats of NIMH,* by Robert C. O'Brien (1971) Fiction Novel [3]
Silkworms	*Project Mulberry Park,* by Linda Sue Park (2005) Fiction [3]
Veterinary Science	*Every Living Thing,* by James Herriot (1992) Fact-based Fiction [3]
Voles	*River Singers, The,* by Tom Moorhouse (2013) Nature, Adventure Fiction [3]
Weasles	*Kine,* by A. R. Lloyd (1982) Nature, Adventure Fiction [3]
Wolves	*Never Cry Wolf,* by Farley Mowat (1963) True Story, Personal Narrative [3]

Advanced Reader: Age 14 to adult
Biology, Animals and Plants [4]

Animal Behavior	**King Solomon's Ring,** by Konrad Lorenz (1949) Nonfiction [4]
Animal Behavior	**Man Meets Dog,** by Konrad Lorenz (1949) Nonfiction [4]
Animal Behavior, Lions	**Born Free,** by Joy Adamson (1960) True Story, Personal Narrative [4]
Botany	**Lab Girl,** by Hope Jahren (2016) Autobiographical True Story [4]
Microbiology	**Microbe Hunters, The,** by Paul de Kruif (1926) Nonfiction [4]
Microbiology, Geology	**Petroplague,** by Amy Rogers (2011) Fiction [4]
Rabbits	**Watership Down,** by Richard Adams (1972) Fiction Novel [4]
Rats	**Rats,** by Robert Sullivan (2004) Personal Experience Nonfiction Story [4]
Spider, Fiction	**Story of Charlotte's Web, The,** by Michael Sims (2011) Nonfiction [4]

Poetry: Biology, Animals and Plants

Animals	**Creatures of Earth, Sea, and Sky,** by Georgia Heard (1992)
Animals	**National Geographic Book of Animal Poetry,** by Patrick Lewis, Editor (2012) Photography
Nature	**Earth, My Likeness: Nature Poetry of Walt Whitman,** by Howard Nelson, Editor (2006)
Nature	**National Geographic Book of Nature Poetry,** by Patrick Lewis, Editor (2015) Photography
Nature	**Poetry for Young People–Robert Frost,** by Gary D. Schmidt, Editor (1994)
Nature	**Robert Frost – Stopping by Woods On A Snowy Evening,** by Robert Frost, Illustrated by Susan Jeffers (1978) Nature Poetry

B.
ECOLOGY, ENVIRONMENT AND EARTH SCIENCE

Early Reader: Ages 5-8 [1]

Conservation	**Dear Greenpeace,** by Simon James (1991) Fiction Picture Book [1]
Conservation, Fable	**Lorax, The,** by Theodore Seuss (1971) Fiction [1]
Ecology	**Wild Woods, The,** by Simon James (1993) Fiction [1]
Geology Fossils	**Mary Anning and The Sea Dragon,** by Jeannine Atkins (2012) Fiction, True Story [1]
Seasons	**Winter is Coming,** by Tony Johnston (2014) Nonfiction [1]

Intermediate Reader: Ages 8-12 [2]

Ecology	**Who Really Killed Cock Robin? An Ecological Mystery,** by Jean Craighead George (1971) Fiction Novel [2]
Geology	**The Earth Dragon Awakes: The San Francisco Earthquake of 1906,** by Laurence Yep (2006) Fact based Fiction [2]
Geology	**Blue John's Cavern, Time Travel Rocks!,** by Tracy Barnhart (2017) Fiction Novel [2]
Geology, Fossils	**Rare Treasure: Mary Anning and Her Remarkable Discoveries,** by Don Brown (1999) Fiction, True Story [2]
Geology fossils	**Time,** by Roger Reid (2011) Fiction Novel [2]

Proficient Reader: Ages 10-13 [3]

Bio-Geography	*Life on Surtsey: Iceland's Upstart Island,* by Loree Burns (2017) Narrative Nonfiction [3]
Environment, Chemistry	*Fuzzy Mud,* by Louis Sachar (2015) Fiction Novel [3]
Sea Otters	*Sea Otter Heroes: The Predators That Saved an Ecosystem,* by Patricia Newman (2017) Nonfiction and Narrative Nonfiction [3]
Weather	*Eye of the Storm,* by Kate Messner (2012) Fiction Novel [3]
Wolves	*Julie of the Wolves,* by Jean Craighead George (1972) Fiction Novel [3]

Advanced Reader: Age 14 to Adult [4]

Conservation Elephants	*Elephant Whisperer, The,* by Lawrence Anthony (2009) True Story, Personal Narrative [4]
Ecology	*Tooth and Claw (2010),* Fiction; Play Script [4]
Geology, Yellowstone	*Ashfall,* by Mike Mullin (2010) Fiction Novel [4]
Global Warming, Oil	*Ship Breaker,* by Paolo Bacigalupi (2010) Fiction Novel [4]
Natural History, Mystery,	*Beyond the Bright Sea,* by Lauren Wolk (2017) Fiction Novel [4]
Water	*Enemy\Flint,* by Diana Burbano (2017) Fact-based Fiction; Play Script [4]

C.
MATH, CHEMISTRY, PHYSICS AND TECHNOLOGY

Early Reader: Ages 5-8 [1]

Computers	*Who Says Women Can't Be Computer Programmers?: The Story of Ada Lovelace,* by Tanya Lee Stone — Biography [1]
Construction	*Mighty, Mighty Construction Site,* by Sherri Duskey Rinker (2017) Picture-book, Fiction [1]
Powered Flight	*Flying Girl, The: How Aida de Acosta Learned to Soar,* by Margarita Engle (2018) True Story [1]
Snow Crystals	*Snowflake Bentley,* by Jacqueline Briggs Martin (1999) Fact-based Fiction [1]
Weight, Balance	*Who Sank the Boat?,* by Pamela Allen (1983) Fiction, Picture Book [1]

Intermediate Reader: Ages 8-12 [2]

Chemistry Atoms	*Adam's Atomic Adventures,* by Alice Baxter (2007) Fiction [2]
Chemistry Elements	*Itch,* by Simon Mayo (2012) Fiction Novel [2]
Computers	*Ada Lovelace, Poet of Science: The First Computer Programmer,* by Diane Stanley (2016) Fact-based Fiction [2]
Fire, Light	*Firework Maker's Daughter, The,* by Philip Pullman (1995) Fantasy Fiction [2]
Math, Concepts	*Matilda,* by Roald Dahl (1988) Fiction Novel [2]

Math, Data	***Tricking the Tallyman,*** by Jacqueline Davies (2014) Fiction [2]
Mechanics	***Clockwork or All Wound Up,*** by Philip Pullman (1996) Fantasy Fiction [2]
Physics, Time	***Tom's Midnight Garden,*** by Philippa Pearce (1958) Fantasy Fiction [2]
Robots, Fiction	***Wild Robot, The,*** by Peter Brown (2016) Fiction Novel [2]

Proficient Reader: Ages 10-13 [3]

DNA, Chemistry	***My Sister Rosalind Franklin: A Family Memoir,*** by Jenifer Glynn (2012) Biography [3]
General Physics	***Adventures of Mr. Thompkins, The, Volume 1,*** by Igor Gamow (2010) Graphic Novel [3]
General Physics	***New World of Mr. Tompkins, The,*** by George Gamow (Author), Russell Stannard (Editor) (1999) Fiction [3]
Light	***Time and Space of Uncle Albert, The,*** by Russell Stannard (1989) Fiction Novel [3]
Math	***Gebra Named Al, A,*** by Wendy Isdell (1993) Fantasy Fiction [3]
Math	***Miscalculations of Lightning Girl, The,*** by Stacy McAnuity (2018) Fiction [3]
Mystery, Experiment	***Sweetness at the Bottom of the Pie, The,*** by Alan Bradley (2009) Fiction Novel [3]

Advanced Reader: Age 14 to adult [4]

Atomic Fission	***Copenhagen,*** by Michael Frayn (1998) Fact-based fiction; Play Script [4]
Biochemistry DNA	***Double Helix, The,*** by James D. Watson (1968) Nonfiction, Biography [4]

Chemistry	*Uncle Tungsten,* by Oliver Sacks (2001) Memoir [4]
Math, Space	*Hidden Figures,* by Margot Lee Shetterly (2016) Fact-based Fiction [4]
Mathematics	*An Abundance of Katherines,* by John Green (2006) Fiction Novel [4]
Mathematics	*Arcadia,* by Tom Stoppard (1973) Fiction; Play Script [4]
Mathematics	*Certain Ambiguity, A: A Mathematical Novel,* by Gaurav Suri and Hartosh Bal (2007) Fiction Novel [4]
Mathematics	*Flatland: A Romance of Many Dimensions,* by Edwin Abbott (1884) Math Fiction [4]
Mathematics	*Proof,* by David Auburn, (2000) Fiction; Play Script [4]
Technology, Electricity	*Last Days of Night, The,* by Graham Moore (2017) Narrative Nonfiction [4]
Nautical	*Boat Who Wouldn't Float, The,* by Farley Mowat (1969) True Story [4]
Particle Physics	*Wizard of Quarks, The,* by Robert Gilmore (2001) Fantasy Fiction [4]
Physics	*Constellations,* by Nick Payne (2012) Fiction; Play Script [4]
Physics	*QED,* by Peter Parnell (2001) Fact-based fiction; Play Script [4]
Technology	*Billion Dollar Molecule,* by Barry Werth, (1995) Nonfiction [4]
Technology	*Practice Effect, The,* by David Brin (1984) Science Fiction [4]

D.

SPACE, TIME TRAVEL, SCIENCE FICTION AND SCIENCE THRILLER

Early Reader: Ages 5-8 [1]

Space Travel	*My Journey to the Stars,* by Scott Kelly (2017) Nonfiction, Autobiographical [1]

Intermediate Reader: Ages 8-12 [2]

Fantasy	*Scarecrow and his Servant, The,* by Philip Pullman (2004) Fairy Tale Fiction [2]
Space Travel Fiction	*Countdown Conspiracy, The,* by Katie Slivensky (2017) Fiction Novel [2]
Space Travel Fiction	*Wonderful Flight to the Mushroom Planet, The,* by Eleanor Cameron (1954) Fiction Novel [2]
Time Travel	*When You Reach Me,* by Rebecca Stead (2009) Fiction Novel [2]
Universe	*George's Secret Key to the Universe,* by Stephen Hawking and Lucy Hawking (2007) Fiction Novel [2]
Astronomy	*Galileo's Journal: 1609-1610,* by Jeanne Pettenati (2006) Fiction [2]

Proficient Reader: Ages 10-13 [3]

Astronomy	*Mary Andromeda and the Amazing Eye,* by J.G. Kemp (2016) Fiction [3]
Astronomy, Newton	*Isaac The Alchemist: Secrets of Isaac Newton, Reveal'd,* by Mary Losure (2017) Narrative Nonfiction [3]

Space, Computers	***Rise of the Rocket Girls,*** by Nathalia Holt (2016) True Stories [3]
Space, Moon Landing	***T-Minus: The Race to the Moon,*** by Jim Ottaviani (2009) True Story, Graphic Novel [3]
Space, Rockets	***Rocket Boys,*** by Homer Hickam (1998) Memoir [3]
Time Travel	***Wrinkle in Time, A,*** by Madeline L'Engle (1962) Fiction Novel [3]

Advanced Reader: Age 14 to Adult [4]

Apocalypse	***Life As We Knew It,*** by Susan Beth Pfeffer (2006) Science Thriller [4]
Astronomy, Galileo	***Galileo's Daughter,*** by Dava Stobel (2000) Nonfiction [4]
Environment Disaster	***40 Signs of Rain,*** by Kim Stanley Robinson (2004) Science Fiction [4]
Science Thriller	***Seeds: a post-apocalyptic adventure,*** by Chris Mandeville (2015) Science Thriller [4]
Space, Mars	***Martian, The,*** by Andy Weir (2012) Science Fiction [4]
Time travel	***3:59,*** by Gretchen McNeil (2013) Science Fiction [4]

So please, oh please, we beg, we pray,
Go throw your tv set away,
And in its place you can install,
a lovely bookshelf on the wall.

—ROALD DAHL

E.
DISCOVERING, INVENTING, AND PROBLEM SOLVING

Early Reader: Ages 5-8 [1]

Einstein	*On a Beam of Light: A Story of Albert Einstein,* by Jennifer Berne (2016) Biography [1]
Invention Fiction	*Moon is Made of Cheese, The,* by Chris and Jenny Kjorness (2016) Fiction Story [1]
Invention Persistence	*Rosie Revere, Engineer,* by Andrea Beaty (2013) Fiction Storybook [1]
Questioning, Experiment	*Ada Twist Scientist,* by Andrea Beaty (2017) Fiction Storybook [1]
Research, Bees	*Humblebee Hunter, The,* by Deborah Hopkinson (2010) Fiction [1]

Intermediate Reader: Ages 8-12 [2]

Invention Fiction	*Frankie Files, The,* by A. J. Ponder (2017) Fiction [2]
Invention Fiction	*Secret Science Alliance and the Copycat Crook, The,* by Eleanor Davis (2009) Graphic Novel [2]
Invention, Toys, Fiction	*Vincent Shadow: Toy Inventor,* by Tim Kehoe (2009) Fiction [2]
Invention, Mechanics, Cars	*Tin Snail, The,* by Cameron McAllister (2014) Fiction [2]
Problem Solving	*Escape from Mr. Lemoncello's Library,* by Chris Grabenstein (2013) Fiction [2]

Research	***Wisdom, the Midway Albatross,*** by Darcy Pattison (2012) Narrative Nonfiction [2]
Careers	***Girls Who Looked Under Rocks,*** by Jeanine Atkins (2000) Nonfiction [2]

Proficient Reader: Ages 10-13 [3]

Mystery, Problem Solving	***Book Scavenger, The,*** by Jennifer Chambliss Bertman (2015) Fiction [3]
Invention	***Boy Who Harnessed The Wind, The,*** by William Kamkwamba, (2012) Nonfiction Novel [3]
Mystery, Detection	***Case of the Missing Moonstone, The (The Wollstonecraft Detective Agency, Book 1),*** by Jordan Stratford (2015) Fiction [3]
Mystery, Problem Solving	***Chasing Vermeer,*** by Blue Balliett (2004) Fiction [3]
Discovery,	***Fourteenth Goldfish, The,*** by Jennifer L. Holm (2014) Fiction Novel [3]
Invention Fiction	***Jack and the Geniuses – At the Bottom of the World,*** by Bill Nye and Gregory Mone (2017) Fiction Novel [3]
Research	***My Season with Penguins: An Antarctic Journal,*** by Sophie Webb (2000) Narrative Nonfiction [3]
Mystery, Problem Solving	***Mysterious Benedict Society, The,*** by Trenton Lee Stewart (2017) Fiction [3]
Mystery, Problem Solving	***Under the Egg,*** by Laura Mars Fitzgerald (2014) Fiction [3]
Mystery, Problem Solving	***Westing Game, The,*** by Ellen Raskin (1978) Fiction [3]
Invention	***What Color Is My World? The Lost History of African-American Inventors,*** by Kareem Abdul-Jabbar (2012) Nonfiction within Fiction [3]

Advanced Reader: Age 14 to Adult [4]

Discovery in Science	**Passion for Science, A,** by Lewis Wolpert and Alison Richards (1988) Nonfiction [4]
Franklin, Rosalind	**Photograph 51,** by Anna Ziegler (2015) Fact-based Fiction; Play Script [4]
Invention	**Farnsworth Invention, The,** by Aaron Sorkin (2007) Fact-based Fiction; Play Script [4]
Neuroscience Brain	**Neurocomic,** by Hana Roš, illustrated by Matteo Farinella (2013) Graphic Novel [4]
Sciences, Concepts	**Science: A Discovery in Comics,** by Margreet de Heer (2012) Nonfiction Graphic Novel [4]
Scientists Conversing	**Dialogues, The,** by Clifford Johnson (2017) Graphic Novel [4]

"The man from whom I caught the addiction to mathematics was a Hungarian University Professor and friend of my father, Dr. Klug. He gave me a 200-year-old book to read when I was eleven years old. The book was entitled 'Algebra'."

—EDWARD TELLER, THEORETICAL PHYSICIST.

F.
ADVENTURING, EXPLORING AND SURVIVING

Intermediate Reader: Ages 8-12 [2]

Adventure, Mystery	*Feather Chase, The,* by Shannon L. Brown (2014) Fiction Novel [2]
Youthful Adventure	*Swallows and Amazons,* by Arthur Ransome (1930) Fiction, Nautical [2]

Proficient Reader: Ages 10-13 [3]

Adventure	*Town Secrets (The Book of Adam 1),* by Scott Gelowitz (2014) Fiction [3]
Adventure Fantasy	*Phantom Tollbooth, The,* by Norton Juster (1961) Fantasy Fiction Adventure Novel, featuring words, and math ideas [3]
Exploration, Survival	*Admiral Richard Byrd,* by Paul Rink (2005) Biography [3]
Forest Survival	*My Side of the Mountain,* by Jean Craighead George (1959) Fiction Novel [3]
Island Survival	*Finding the Lone Woman of San Nicolas Island,* by R.C. Nidever (2017) Nonfiction Novel [3]
Island Survival	*Island of the Blue Dolphins,* by Scott O'Dell (1960) Nonfiction Novel [3]
Math Adventure	*Island of the Unknowns: A Mystery,* by Benedict Carey (2011) Fiction [3]
Wilderness Survival	*Hatchet,* by Gary Paulsen (1987) Fiction Novel [3]

Advanced Reader: Age 14 to adult [4]

Airships, Adventure	***Airborn,*** by Kenneth Oppel (2004) Steampunk Fiction Novel [4]
Exploration	***On The Verge,*** by Eric Overmeyer (1985) Fiction, time travel; Play Script [4]
Arctic Exploration	***Voyage of the Narwhal, The,*** by Andrea Barrett (1998) Fiction Novel [4]

G.
MISCELLANEOUS

Science and Nature	***Archangel,*** by Andrea Barrett (2013) Fiction, Short Stories [4]
Science and Nature	***Servants of the Map,*** by Andrea Barrett (2002) Fiction, Short Stories [4]
Science and Nature	***Shell Collector, The,*** by Anthony Doerr (2001) Fiction, Short Stories [4]
Science and Nature	***Ship Fever,*** by Andrea Barrett (1996) Fiction, Short Stories [4]
Poetry	***Tree That Time Built, The: A Celebration of Nature, Science, and Imagination,*** by Mary Ann Hoberman (2009)
Poetry	***Brain Juice, Science Fresh Squeezed,*** by Carol Diggery Shields (2003)
Poetry	***Poetry of Science,*** Compiled by Sylvia Vardell and Janet Wong (2015)
Poetry	***Spectacular Science,*** selected by Lee Bennett Hopkins (1999) Poetry

AFTERWORD

"To read is to fly: it is to soar to a point of vantage which gives a view over wide terrains of history, human variety, ideas, shared experience and the fruits of many inquiries." —A.C. Grayling MA, DPhil (Oxon) British philosopher and author.

On the other hand, Plato's words on writing are worth contemplating: " If men learn this, it will implant forgetfulness in their souls; they will cease to exercise memory because they rely on that which is written, calling things to remembrance no longer from within themselves, but by means of external marks."

Burying myself in a book was something I greatly enjoyed as youngster growing up during World War II in the UK. I still value and enjoy reading as a daily pastime. Curiously, my memories of the books I read are shadowy. Even the memories of books recently finished. Instead of specifics I tend to recall where I was, how I felt while reading the stories, what the books felt or smelled like, and whether a book is somehow personally significant for me. However, memories do exist since when I pick up and open the pages of a book that I've enjoyed, the illustrations and the words of the text are immediately familiar even after many months or years.

In his amazing and eminently readable tome, *A History of Reading*, Alberto Manguel writes, "I think I read in at least two ways. First, by following, breathlessly, the events and characters without stopping to notice the details, the quickening pace of reading sometimes hurtling the story beyond the last page. ...Secondly, by careful exploration, scrutinizing the text to understand its raveled meaning, finding pleasure merely in the sound of the words..." Manguel relates too the experience, that I share, that sometimes it is the physical book as well as its much loved story that remains as a beguiling memory. He writes, "One reads a certain edition, a specific copy, recognizable by the roughness or smoothness of the paper, by its scent, by a slight tear on page 71 and a coffee ring on the right-hand corner of the back cover."

Strong impressions, but foggy memories, of books that I read when I was about nine or ten include *At the Back of the North Wind* (MacDonald), *Lord Jim* (Conrad), *The Wonderful Adventures of Nils* (Lagerlöf) and Arthur Ransome's *Swallows and Amazons* series. I read and re-read all twelve of Ransome's stories featuring youthful adventure, a love of wildlife, all things nautical, courage, teamwork and resourcefulness. Enduring echoes of these particular stories reflect my adult feelings about what is important in my life.

A favorite of the Ransome books for me was *Coot Club*, in which two preteen siblings join 'The Coot Club' formed by a group of local children to protect local birds and their nests from egg collectors and other disturbances. Observation of and attention to the preservation of the wildlife of the lake and rivers where the children sailed their boats was a continuing, underlying theme throughout the series. This clearly resonated with me and has stayed with me as I eventually studied science and became a biology teacher.

My other childhood joy was to spend my considerable hours of unsupervised, spare time outside school wandering in search of things to record in my nature diary. I recorded observations of all sorts about the world around me, on the streets or in the long stretches of Port Meadow close to my Oxford home. I charted the weather daily noting the effects of the sun, wind and rain on plants and animals as I did so. I described and drew things I saw or collected. Some smaller collected pieces became physical parts of the diary. An amalgam of observation, science, and art activities, the creation of the diary and its associated wandering activities was, like reading, a significant part of my growing up.

My nature diary enterprise reflects an essential aspect of science and of the mission of the Explorit Science Center I co-founded and led years ago—curiosity, observation, and investigation through the consideration of "What?", "Where?", "Why?" and "What if?" types of questions. Children, parents, and teachers using the *To Read Is To Fly* booklist might find the combination of reading with a complementary activity involving inquiry very satisfying as I did.

BOOKS AND BUTTERFLIES!

The butterfly motif you see throughout this book is a visual metaphor for the "Butterfly Effect"...when small events like the flapping of a butterfly's wings—or the reading of a book—lead to much larger events.

The notion of a "Butterfly Effect" was born in 1972 when that pioneer of chaos theory, Edward Lorenz, posed the question, "Does the flap of a butterfly's wings in Brazil set off a tornado in Texas?" The science may be questionable, but the concept of the "Butterfly Effect" caught the popular imagination.

I thought about titling this book "Butterfly Effects," hoping that reading stories like those featured here might inspire big thinking and action in the future lives of readers. The title changed, but the hope lingers...and the butterfly illustrations are the symbol of my hope.

CAVEAT

This little book is about encouraging reading to inspire interest, enjoyment and familiarity with science and nature but I would be remiss if I did not also strongly encourage intimate, personal involvement with our natural surroundings.

I recently read what Dave Goulson (Professor of Biological Sciences at Sussex University UK[1]) has to say about the large majority of children who grow out of their fascination with nature by about the age of eight and no longer see the natural world as in any way personally relevant to them.

Goulson suggests that the change comes about when children get too few opportunities in our modern, urbanized world to regularly interact with nature. He notes that they cannot learn to love something they do not know. For example, a staggering 80% of the U.S and 82% of the UK populations now live in urban areas. Many children in such circumstances in the U.S and Britain today do not explore and investigate beyond their homes at the wildlife edges of town as I and other children of my era did. A child who has never been lucky enough to wander through a wildflower meadow in late spring to smell the flowers, hear the birds and insect songs and watch butterflies flit amongst the grass is unlikely to care much if such natural areas disappear.

Even if the casual freedom of past times can no longer exist it is still possible for individuals, families and school classes to experience the natural world on a regular basis if they wish. Such places still exist and are available to the public. Additionally, many families live in locations where their gardens can offer wonderful opportunities for grubbing around in the soils to grow vegetables, fruits and flowers or discover amazing varieties of plant and animal wildlife.

The possibilities for learning to love nature do exist but in our current times they need to be more regularly, actively and purposefully sought out.

So, my heartfelt admonition dear reader, is for you to engage both in reading about the natural world and in interacting with the real thing as much as possible.

1. Goulson, Dave, (2017). Bee Quest. London SW1V 2SA: Jonathan Cape, Penguin Random House